FOOL'S P.

A Farcical Comedy in Three Acts

by

PETER COKE

SAMUEL FRENCH

LONDON
NEW YORK   TORONTO   SYDNEY   HOLLYWOOD

ISBN 0 573 01137 0

MADE AND PRINTED IN GREAT BRITAIN BY
LATIMER TREND AND CO. LTD, PLYMOUTH

MADE IN ENGLAND

FOOL'S PARADISE

Produced at the Apollo Theatre, London, on the 1st April 1959, with the following cast of characters:

(in the order of their appearance)

JULIUS CAXTON	*Guy Deghy*
ROSE	*Eileen Draycott*
SUSAN DAWSON	*Jennifer Daniel*
CATHERINE HAYLING	*Nora Swinburne*
JANE HAYLING	*Cicely Courtneidge*
PHILIP HAYLING	*Ronald Wilson*
FIONA RENSHAW	*Pamela Strong*
BRIGETTE BLAIR	*Agnes Lauchlan*

Directed by ALLAN DAVIS
Setting by TONY WALTON

SYNOPSIS OF SCENES

The action of the Play passes in the drawing-room of the Haylings' house in Westminster

ACT I
4 p.m. on a Monday in May

ACT II
A few days later. Seven o'clock in the evening

ACT III
The following Wednesday afternoon

Time—the present

To face page 1 "Fool's Paradise"

ACT I

Scene—*The drawing-room of the Haylings' house in Westminster. Four p.m. on a Monday in May.*

Although faded and cluttered with antiques, it is a perfectly proportioned Georgian room, on the first floor, with an only door up L, leading to a small landing and a curved staircase. A large bay window up R has a distant view of part of Buckingham Palace and the Victoria Memorial. There are built-in shelves R and a window-seat. A large sofa is LC with an oval table in front of it. An ornate desk is RC with a chair behind it and a stool in front of it. There is a telephone on the desk. A bureau stands down R. There are upright chairs R, L and up C, and an armchair down R. Against the wall down L there is a console table with a small round table above it. At night the room is lit by a chandelier pendant C and a standard lamp up R. The switch for the standard lamp is on the lamp itself, and the switch for the chandelier is below the door up L. On the landing there is a pedestal and an upright chair.

When the Curtain *rises,* Julius Caxton *is alone in the room, sitting on the sofa, studying the contents of the room with an appraising eye. He is a fleshy, balding, easily-excited man, wearing thickly-rimmed spectacles and too well-cut clothes. He has an accent which becomes marked when he is upset. After a few moments, he rises, goes to the door, opens it a little, listens a moment, then moves below the door and looks at a flower-painting hanging high on the wall. Being too short to reach it, he spreads his handkerchief on the chair underneath the picture to avoid footmarks, stands on the chair, takes a small torch from his pocket and with its aid, searches for the signature, slightly tilting the picture as he does so.*

Rose (*off; calling*) All right, I'll tell her to wait.

(Caxton *gets hastily off the chair, gathers up his handkerchief and sits on the sofa. After a moment, as no-one comes in, he rises, crosses to the heavy ormulu-mounted bureau down R, and examines it carefully. To see the state of the back, he moves it slightly away from the wall. As he does so, an ormulu mount on the downstage corner drops to the floor.* Caxton *is alarmed and tries to replace it, but it will not stick. He finds one of the screws on the floor, but still cannot attach the piece. In desperation he takes off his shoe and hammers with it.* Rose's *voice is heard again*)

(*Off*) Come up here, miss, and sit down.

(Caxton *hastily replaces his shoe and sits in the armchair down R.*
 . Rose *enters up L and stands in the doorway. She is an ancient parlour-maid with a rusty voice and a firm manner*)

(*Accusingly*) What was that banging?

CAXTON (*innocently*) I didn't hear anything.

ROSE. I've always said this room's haunted.

CAXTON. Haunted?

ROSE. Well, it couldn't have been woodpeckers, could it? (*She turns to the hall and calls*) In here, miss; you'll have to join the queue. (*She stands above the open door*)

(SUSAN DAWSON *enters. She is charming, young, frank, and simply dressed.* CAXTON *rises*)

SUSAN (L *of Rose*) Thank you. Will Mrs Hayling be long?

ROSE. I'd rather guess the weather.

CAXTON (*moving* C; *tetchily*) But my time's money. I've been waiting ten minutes already.

ROSE (*crossing to* L *of Caxton*) Whooh!

(SUSAN *moves above the left end of the sofa and puts down her handbag and gloves*)

When you've lived as long as I have you'll know the unimportance of ten minutes. How old do you think I am?

CAXTON. I didn't come to take part in a quiz programme.

ROSE (*to Susan; cackling*) You, then. What's your guess?

SUSAN. Well—er, I'm a very bad judge of ages.

ROSE (*delightedly*) Getting on for eighty. That's me! Getting on for eighty. (*She notices the crooked picture* L)

CAXTON. Well, now we've happily settled that vital question, what about my appointment?

ROSE. Who was it you wanted to see?

CAXTON (*annoyed*) Is it my tongue or your ears?

(ROSE *crosses above the sofa to the chair* L)

(*Very distinctly*) Mrs Hayling.

SUSAN. I think she means which Mrs Hayling.

CAXTON. Is there more than one? The owner of the house, then.

ROSE (*enjoying herself*) That's no help. (*She stands on the chair and straightens the picture*)

CAXTON. The widow of Mr Basil Hayling, then.

ROSE (*convulsed*) Neither's that. (*She gets down from the chair*)

CAXTON (*very annoyed*) Why not? They can't both be the widows of Mr Basil Hayling.

SUSAN. I think you'll find they are.

CAXTON (*amazed*) And both now live here—together?

ROSE (*crossing to* L *of Caxton*) They have to. He left the house to the two of them—hoping they'd drive each other mad. (*She cackles*) Sense of humour, that's what Mr Basil had. That's why I'm over eighty; sense of humour and enough salts to cover a sixpence every morning. (*She crosses below Caxton to the bureau and fixes the corner piece*)

SUSAN (*to Caxton*) Perhaps I could help you; I know them both.

ROSE. Mrs Jane's out, anyhow. And Mrs Catherine's writing

her novel, and mustn't be disturbed while she's in the mood.

CAXTON (*acidly*) Is the mood likely to last much longer?

ROSE. She didn't have any lunch, so the clatter of tea-things'll bring her to her senses.

CAXTON (*moving to L of Rose*) Couldn't you clatter them now?

ROSE (*flatly*) No, I could not.

CAXTON (*looking at his watch*) I've got a further call in this district; I'd better fit that in. (*He crosses to the door and picks up his bag*)

(ROSE *moves up* C)

(*He returns to L of Rose and presses a coin into her hand*) Here; and there'll be another if you brew up in the next half hour.

(CAXTON *crosses and exits.* ROSE *follows to the door and looks after Caxton.* SUSAN *moves down L of the door*)

ROSE (*watching from the door*) Think he'll pinch anything?

SUSAN. Oh, surely not.

ROSE (*moving up R of Susan*) If so, hope it's that carved ivory thing; awful dust-trap.

SUSAN. Who is he?

ROSE. Haven't the foggiest. For that matter—I don't know who you are.

SUSAN. I'm Susan Dawson, and I've come to . . .

(SUSAN *breaks off as a ball of paper, wrapped round a bunch of keys is thrown from upstairs, whizzes through the door and lands between the sofa and the desk*)

What's that?

ROSE (*moving* C *and picking up the package*) It's all right. I know. It's Mrs Catherine.

(SUSAN *crosses to L of Rose*)

She's always throwing messages in. (*She opens the paper, reads it, then crosses to the door and shouts up the stairs*) Yes, he *has* gone.

(SUSAN *moves to L of the desk*)

CATHERINE (*off*) Oh, thank goodness. Why didn't you tell me immediately?

(CATHERINE HAYLING *enters and stands just inside the open doorway,* L *of Rose.* CATHERINE *is a tall, dark, good-looking woman who dresses well, but a little eccentrically. She carries her spectacles and a pencil*)

(*Anxiously*) Was he from the worm people?

ROSE. Don't know where he was from.

CATHERINE. Well, did he look like a bailiff?

ROSE. He didn't have an apron on.

SUSAN. He didn't look like one to me.

CATHERINE (*crossing to L of Susan*) Mrs Dawson! I'm so sorry, I didn't know you were here.

Rose. I told you she was five minutes ago.

Catherine. You only speak the truth when it causes maximum embarrassment. (*She crosses to* R *of Rose*) Go and get the tea. Give me your hand. (*She takes Rose's hand, and marks it with her pencil*) "T." (*To Susan*) To remind her what she's going for.

(Rose, *looking at the palm of her hand, exits, leaving the door open*)

(*She crosses to* L *of Susan*) I apologize for this muddle, dear. But the swindling firm who did our wood-worm in the staircase threaten us with the bailiffs. And as we've no idea what bailiffs look like, anyone we don't expect, we suspect.

Susan. I won't keep you a moment. It's just that your son told me that you'd let your two upstairs rooms to anyone who'd help in the house.

Catherine. You can't want to?

Susan. I do.

Catherine (*delighted*) Come and sit down, quickly.

(Susan *crosses and sits on the sofa.* Catherine *moves down*

Susan. You see, the lease of my flat's ended, and I'm desperate for somewhere to live.

Catherine. And we're desperate for help. Basil left us this enormous house and not a penny to run it. We'd welcome you if you're absolutely sure.

Susan. I am, but I expect you want to know . . .

Catherine. I don't want to know anything. (*She moves and puts her pencil and spectacles on the desk*) As a writer I can tell immediately, and you look admirable to me. (*She moves* C. *Doubtfully*) The trouble is I'm sure we won't to you.

Susan. I think we'll get on very well.

Catherine. I'm afraid you may find the rooms rather odd. Jane bought the furniture at an auction, by mistake. The bed's covered in dragons.

Susan (*smiling*) I shan't mind; I'm very fond of animals.

Catherine. And the wallpaper's peeling off a bit. (*She moves to the armchair down* R *and sits*) Still, if Jane sells the emeralds for as much as . . . (*She suddenly breaks off*) Did you hear that?

Susan. About the emeralds?

Catherine. You did! How awful, no-one's supposed to know.

Susan. I'll pretend I didn't hear.

Catherine. No, I don't want you to think I'm deceitful before you even move in. It's just that the emeralds . . . (*She suddenly breaks off again*) Oh, I might as well tell you all about them—having gone so far. (*She rises, crosses to the door, closes it then stands* L *of the sofa*) Only don't breathe a word, will you?

Susan. Of course not.

Catherine. It's all terribly exciting. Basil—Jane's and my late husband—had an old sister, and to our great delight she's just died. I don't mean that. We weren't delighted because we didn't know she'd left us anything. (*She crosses above the sofa to the desk*) I don't mean that, either. What I'm trying to say is—after the poor thing did die, we found she *had* left us something. (*She sits on the stool* L *of the desk*)

SUSAN. No wonder you're excited.

CATHERINE. We hoped she would, because she always felt guilty for not having stopped us marrying her brother.

SUSAN. Should she have?

CATHERINE. It would have been kinder. Basil was the dearest man in the world, of course. The trouble was he was dear to too many of the female part of it at the same time.

SUSAN. I see.

CATHERINE. So Alice left us this incredible spray of Indian emeralds as a form of compensation.

SUSAN. Very rich compensation.

CATHERINE. Yes, and they may be worth quite a lot because she got them from a Maharaja she nursed in—wherever he was Maharaja of—I forget now. She saved him from losing his finger, or his toe, or something he wanted to keep.

SUSAN (*rising and moving to* L *of Catherine*) Do let me see them.

CATHERINE. I can't. (*She rises*) It was far too elaborate for us to wear, so Jane's taken it off to a jeweller who advertises as giving the highest prices. And we're hoping to settle all our debts. (*She moves to the window*)

(SUSAN *moves up* L *of the desk*)

What can have happened to her? Never mind. (*She crosses to the bell-push below the door and presses it*) I'll get Rose to show you the rooms while you're waiting.

SUSAN. Thank you.

CATHERINE (*conspiratorially*) Only whatever you do, don't mention the emeralds to Philip. He knows nothing about them, and would immediately demand half the money to pay his debts. And Jane and I must pay ours first.

SUSAN. I won't mention it to a soul.

CATHERINE. I was mad to let Jane go alone. When she's excited she's quite remarkably unreliable. (*She crosses to the window*) Heaven knows what she may have got up to.

SUSAN (*moving up* L *of the sofa*) I'm sure you've no need to worry. (*She picks up her bag and gloves*)

CATHERINE. My dear, when Jane's about, there's always need to worry.

(ROSE *enters and stands by the door*)

ROSE. You'll kill me if you keep bringing me up those stairs.

(*The telephone rings.* CATHERINE *goes to the desk, lifts the receiver and covers the mouthpiece*)

CATHERINE (*to Rose*) This is Mrs Dawson, Rose. If you're nice she's going to live upstairs and help you at odd times.

ROSE (*to Susan*) You'll regret it, dear. But come on.

(ROSE *and* SUSAN *exit, closing the door behind them*)

CATHERINE (*into the telephone*) Hullo? . . . Which Mrs Hayling—Mrs Jane or Mrs Catherine? . . . Oh. Well, I'm expecting her any time . . .

(*The sound of a door slam is heard off*)

Wait a moment, that's probably her. Who is it speaking? . . . (*Dismayed*) Oh . . . But I'm sure she sent you a cheque months ago . . How odd . . . Well, I'm afraid you'll have to wait because she's gone abroad for several weeks—good-bye. (*She hastily replaces the receiver, moves* R *of the desk and makes a note*)

(JANE HAYLING *enters, closing the door behind her. She is a sparkling, exuberant woman, with so much enthusiasm that she never has time to think. She carries a tall rubber plant in a pot, and three smart carrier bags*)

JANE. Catherine, I've been insulted! What do you think the taxi-man just called me?
CATHERINE. What?
JANE. What Basil often used to call you. (*She moves above the sofa and puts her carrier bags on it*)
CATHERINE. Jane!
JANE. Never mind, I had my revenge. I called him what Basil often used to call me.
CATHERINE (*crossing below the desk to* C) But why all this filthy language?
JANE (*crossing with the plant to* L *of Catherine*) Because this made a little puddle on his back seat.
CATHERINE. What is it?
JANE (*dumping the plant into Catherine's hands*) A present for you.
CATHERINE. I don't want it. (*She returns the plant to Jane*)
JANE. Yes, you do. (*She hands the plant to Catherine*) And enjoy it properly; I paid cash for it. (*She moves to the sofa and takes a wool stole from a carrier bag*) I've bought you another lovely present, too. Something absolutely made for you. (*She crosses and drapes the stole around Catherine*) There. If you look closely you'll see the moths have been at it here and there. But I got it at half price, and as they've eaten less than half it's an absolute bargain.
CATHERINE. Thank you. It's lovely. (*Excitedly*) Do all these presents mean you've sold the emeralds?
JANE (*gaily ignoring the question*) I bought myself a present, too: this wonderfully impractical coat. (*She crosses down* R *and spins around*) What do you think of it?
CATHERINE. Nothing half-price about that. It must have cost a fortune.
JANE. Don't worry; I didn't have to pay for it. (*She moves to* R *of Catherine and slightly lowers her voice*) I had the most amazing luck.

A *new* man served me who didn't know about our little troubles with the account. He was an absolute poppet. He let me have these shoes, as well. (*She limps down* LC) They're absolute agony, but aren't they gorgeous?

CATHERINE. How much did they cost?

JANE. Ten pounds.

CATHERINE (*horrified*) Ten pounds! But we haven't a penny. (*She brightens*) But I suppose we have now. How much did you get for the emeralds?

JANE (*moving to* L *of Catherine*) I had a terrible time even finding the jeweller's shop. You'd think number fifteen would be next to number fourteen, wouldn't you? But, oh, no! Fourteen—then sixteen. And where do you think fifteen was? (*She moves to* L *of the table* LC) Miles away the other side of the road, next to the fish shop. They had the most heavenly lobsters on the slab. I was dying to buy two but I only had fourpence in my bag . . .

CATHERINE (*interrupting*) Never mind the lobsters, what about the emeralds? (*She puts the plant on the table* LC)

JANE (*moving to* L *of Catherine*) Well, when I eventually found the jeweller's, who do you think I met coming out?

CATHERINE (*removing the stole and moving up* C) I don't care who you met coming out. (*She puts the stole on the chair up* C)

JANE. You will when you hear who it was. Brigette Blair.

CATHERINE (*moving to* R *of Jane; delighted*) Brigette! I haven't seen her for ages. How is she?

JANE. As peculiar as ever. Terrified of catching cold. All I could see was a nose sticking out of a pile of shawls.

CATHERINE. Perhaps it's just as well we haven't seen her for ages.

JANE. The ages have come to an end. (*She crosses to the mirror down* L *and removes her hat*) She's having dinner with us next week.

CATHERINE. Oh, Jane, you know we can't afford to have people to dinner.

JANE. She—and her son.

CATHERINE (*making a face*) Oh, not James Blair, too? He's a revolting young man.

JANE (*correcting*) He's an extremely nice young man.

CATHERINE. Since when?

JANE. Since this morning, when I heard he's now a TV producer.

CATHERINE (*incredulously*) James Blair?

JANE (*moving to* L *of Jane; excitedly*) It's quite wonderful. He remembered I was an actress before I married Basil, and said why didn't I make a come-back on the television.

CATHERINE. He said that?

JANE. Well, maybe I put the idea in his head. Anyway, that's why they're coming to dinner. (*She puts her handbag on the stool then puts her hat on the chair up* C)

CATHERINE (*acidly*) Does he know you only played maids? *Silent* maids at that?

JANE. If I could do so much without words, imagine what I'll be like when I have them. Though I'd better polish up my mime and elocution before next week. (*She moves up* L *and declaims with gestures*) "Oh, let no noble eye profane a tear . . ."

CATHERINE (*moving to* R *of Jane*) No, no, not now, Jane. For pity's sake, tell me about the emeralds.

JANE (*joyously*) TV salaries are enormous; we shall be able to pay off all our debts.

CATHERINE (*slowly and loudly*) Have you, or have you not, sold the emeralds?

JANE (*moving below the sofa*) I've brought you another lovely present. (*She takes a bottle of crème de menthe from a carrier*) Your favourite *crème de menthe*.

CATHERINE (*moving above the sofa*) I don't want *crème de menthe*.

JANE. You will! (*Ashamedly*) I haven't sold the emeralds. (*She puts the bottle in Catherine's hands and moves below the desk*)

CATHERINE (*moving* C) Jane! Why not?

JANE. Well, at first glance he said they might be worth two or three thousand pounds . . .

CATHERINE. Two or three thousand!

JANE. Then he took a longer glance, and changed pounds to pence.

CATHERINE. Only pence! But why?

JANE (*moving to* R *of Catherine*) Some idiot's painted the backs of the stones with green varnish. It makes them a wonderful colour they aren't.

CATHERINE. But surely emeralds are valuable whatever's been done to their backs?

JANE. He says they're probably worthless beryls. Evidently Indian court jewellers splashed green paint on to any old stones if they knew they were going to be given away as gifts. (*She removes her coat and puts it on the window-seat*)

CATHERINE. It's terrible. Let me look at them.

JANE. I left them with our Polish watchmaker.

CATHERINE. He wouldn't know anything about emeralds.

JANE (*moving to* R *of Catherine*) Not to sell them. To mend the pin. (*Proudly*) I shall wear them for my first appearance on TV.

(CATHERINE *moves to the sofa, puts the carriers over the back of it and sits*)

CATHERINE. You won't be able to appear if you're locked up for debt.

JANE. We shan't be locked up. Have a little faith, Catherine. (*She crosses to the light switch below the door*) Have they cut off the light? (*She switches the chandelier on and off*) The dears! (*She crosses to the desk*) What about the telephone? (*She lifts the receiver and listens*) No, still clicking away quite happily. (*She replaces the receiver*)

CATHERINE. But for how long? And now the emeralds valueless. (*Despairingly*) What are we going to do?

Jane (*picking up her handbag and crossing to* R *of the sofa*) Go out and buy two ridiculous hats that neither of us dare wear.

Catherine. We haven't the money to buy a hatpin.

Jane. That's just the time to spend money—when you haven't got it. It makes shopping so exciting.

Catherine. You drive me mad with your absurdly optimistic attitude.

Jane. It's the only sensible attitude. (*She sits in the armchair down* R) If things are going to turn out badly, worrying won't help. So why not be hopefully happy in the meantime.

(Philip Hayling *enters. He is a light-hearted young man, attractive in an untidy way. He carries a string of Spanish onions*)

Philip (*poking his head round the door*) Anyone not like onions?

Catherine. What?

Philip (*coming in and closing the door*) Well, whether you do or not, you've got them. (*He crosses to* R *of the sofa and holds out the onions to Catherine*) With all my love, Mother darling.

Catherine. Why have you been buying onions?

Philip (*putting the onions on the floor behind the sofa*) I wanted to show off my French to the chap selling them at the door. (*He crosses to the desk, takes a cigarette from the box on it, and lights it*)

Jane. He's doing well! He sold me two bunches.

Catherine. If you don't both *stop* practising your French we'll have to open a vegetable shop.

Philip (*crossing to* C; *a little too casually*) I saw Mrs Dawson as I came in. What do you think of her?

Catherine. She's sweet. Jane, that nice Mrs Dawson's taking the rooms upstairs.

Jane. Miracles aren't over.

Catherine (*suddenly gloomy*) Though now we'd better set about finding a tenant for the attic.

Philip (*worried*) Why? You said things had taken a turn for the better.

Jane. They've whizzed back again.

Philip. Don't tell me we're at another financial crisis?

Jane. At and beyond.

Catherine. We're practically at the door of the debtors' prison.

Philip (*upset*) Oh, no.

Jane. Why?

Philip (*guardedly*) I—I wanted to talk to you about something.

Catherine. If it concerns money—don't.

Philip. But it's something very important to me, Mother. (*He moves to* R *of Catherine. Impatiently*) I think I'd better give up trying to get a degree, find a job and earn some money.

Catherine. You'll do nothing of the sort. We've scraped to make you an engineering genius . . .

(Jane *takes out her compact and powders her nose*)

JANE. And that's what you're going to be—even if we only see you on visiting days, through bars.

PHILIP (*moving up* L *of Jane*) But, Jane, by the time I qualify I shall have father's legacy. (*Urgently*) There must be some way of getting that money before I'm thirty.

CATHERINE. Possibly, *if* we had hundreds to toss to the legal sharks.

PHILIP (*looking around the room*) Dare we risk selling something?

JANE. Selling something!

CATHERINE. You know the furniture's tied up even tighter than your legacy.

JANE. It would be madness, anyhow. The reason we go on getting credit is because of all this furniture. (*She waves her hand around*) It impresses the tradesmen. The window-cleaner was only saying the other day how safe it made him feel.

(ROSE *enters*)

ROSE. He's here again.

JANE. Why is it no-one has a name nowadays?

ROSE. Because they mumble.

CATHERINE (*alarmed*) It's the bailiffs.

(PHILIP *moves up* L *of the desk*)

(*She rises and crosses down* R *of Philip*) Philip, go and push him out.

ROSE. It's about some vases.

CATHERINE (*crossing below Philip to* R *of Rose*) Vases?

JANE. Vases? Oh, vases! (*She rises and puts her handbag on the stool*) It must be Mr Caxton. He's going to turn them into an electric blanket. Show him up, Rose.

(ROSE *exits, closing the door behind her*)

PHILIP (*moving to* L *of Jane; slowly*) What? Who? Why? And how?

JANE. Don't be so pernickety. (*She moves to the chair* R, *stands on it and takes two vases from the shelves*)

(PHILIP *moves and assists Jane*)

You remember these ghastly vases Brigette Blair gave us when she had her end-of-the-world phase?

CATHERINE (*moving up* C) I remember she got over it before she gave away anything good.

JANE (*putting the vases on the desk*) Well, when I was in this man's antique shop, he said how difficult it was to get stock.

(PHILIP *moves to* R *of Catherine*)

And I thought how difficult it was to keep warm in bed. (*She points triumphantly to the vases and makes a conjurer's "pass"*) So! Cold vases into warm sheets! Do you think he might give us thirty bob for them?

CATHERINE. Not unless he's blind.

JANE. Well, a pound, anyhow. Then if I put it on a horse at five to one I can buy an electric blanket.

(ROSE *enters and stands above the doorway*)

ROSE (*announcing*) Mr Caxton.

(CAXTON *enters, carrying his bag.*
  ROSE *exits, closing the door behind her*)

CAXTON (*beaming*) Quite a reception committee, now, eh?

JANE (*crossing to Caxton*) Good afternoon, Mr Caxton. How nice of you to come. (*She looks at his bag*) Are you staying the night?

CAXTON. Just a bag for the goods.

JANE. Oh, good. This is Catherine Hayling, and her son Philip.

(CAXTON *puts his bag down* L, *then crosses below Jane to Catherine and shakes hands with her.* JANE *stands above the sofa*)

CAXTON. Pleased to meet you, dear—(*he hastily corrects himself*) Mrs Hayling. (*To Philip*) And you.

PHILIP. Thank you.

CAXTON (*moving down* C *and looking around*) I must congratulate you on your belongings. (*He crosses down* L) Some very good stuff you've got in here.

CATHERINE. How nice of you.

CAXTON. I hope you don't let your domestic bang about when she cleans?

CATHERINE. She hardly ever does.

CAXTON (*touching the beautifully carved mirror on the wall down* L) This, for instance: it could be ruined.

CATHERINE (*warningly*) Careful!

JANE. The wire's a bit rusty.

CAXTON. I suppose you know it's valuable?

JANE. My husband gave it to me in Venice. (*To Catherine*) When I found out about that Contessa.

(CAXTON *crosses to* L *of the table* LC *and looks closely at it*)

(*She moves to* L *of Caxton*) That came from Paris, for almost the same reason.

CAXTON. Very nice, too. (*Hastily*) Though when I say nice or valuable, don't let it raise your hopes. (*He crosses to the bureau down* R) They wouldn't fetch anything in a sale-room.

PHILIP. How lucky they're not going to a sale-room, then.

CAXTON. But your stuff certainly makes my professional saliva run.

JANE (*sotto voce*) Disgusting!

CAXTON (*moving to the standard lamp and switching it on*) Still, first things first, eh? (*He turns to the desk*) Are those the vases?

JANE (*crossing to* L *of Caxton*) Oh, yes. Those are the vases. (*Airily*) We were just discussing whether they were Ming or Tang.

CAXTON (*sitting in the desk chair*) I hope you're not going to be pricey because I want to make a deal. (*He examines the vases*) Oh, I don't know. Not up to much, are they? (*He takes a magnifying glass from his pocket and examines the bottom of a vase*)

JANE (*pointing it out*) That little anchor makes them very valuable, I'm sure.

CAXTON. No, no, it just means they were made for an admiral. (*He rings the vases with the handle of his magnifying glass to test whether they are cracked*)

JANE (*pointing to the shelves*) I'll get down those two; then we can play *Auld Lang Syne*.

CAXTON. How much do you want, dear—Mrs Hayling?

JANE. Well . . .

PHILIP. You're the buyer; you name the price.

CAXTON. Well, I want to be absolutely honest with you. Give me an idea what you're expecting.

JANE. Well—we're expecting . . .

PHILIP. If you don't want to make an offer, let's cancel the whole transaction.

CAXTON (*rising and moving* R *of the desk*) No, no, we don't want to do that.

JANE (*moving above the desk*) No, we don't want to do that.

CAXTON. At a rough guess I would say they're worth about— (*hopefully*) twenty pounds?

JANE (*sitting in the desk chair; staggered*) Twenty pounds!

CAXTON (*thinking Jane is surprised at the smallness of the offer*) Twenty-two, at the most.

JANE (*almost speechless*) Twenty-two, at the most. (*She rises and is about to offer the vases to Caxton*)

PHILIP (*quickly realizing the vases are valuable*) If that's your best we must certainly cancel the transaction. (*He picks up the vases*)

CAXTON. No, no, we don't want to do that.

JANE (*taking the vases from Philip and putting them on the right end of the desk near Caxton*) No, no, we don't want to do that. (*She sits in the desk chair*)

CAXTON. Maybe that's a slight undervaluation now I come to look at them again. Tell me what you want.

PHILIP. At least fifty pounds.

CAXTON. Fifty pounds! I'd sooner put it in the collection plate.

JANE (*imitating Caxton*) No, no, we don't want to do that.

PHILIP. It's your turn, then.

CAXTON. I'm a sentimental fool, and I'll lose by it, but I'll go as far as thirty.

JANE. I think we should . . .

PHILIP (*picking up the vases and moving towards the shelves*) Put them away again. I agree.

(CAXTON *takes the vases from Philip and replaces them on the desk*)

CAXTON (*very excited*) No, no, no! Not that I'd as much as look at them if stock wasn't so hard to get. I'll give you my final offer.

Thirty-two. And a mangle won't get any more out of me.

JANE (*rising; to Philip*) A mangle won't get any more out of him.

PHILIP. Then we'd better accept.

JANE (*to Caxton*) But our terms are strictly C.O.D. And there's no D. until I have the C.

(ROSE *enters carrying a tray of tea-things.*

SUSAN *follows her on, carrying a cake-stand.* ROSE *puts the tray on the table* LC. SUSAN *puts the cake-stand* R *of the table* LC. CATHERINE *sits* C *of the sofa.* PHILIP *moves up* C)

ROSE (*to Susan*) Thank you, my dear. It's very kind of you.

JANE (*moving to* L *of the desk*) Ah, Mrs—er—we've got you, I hear.

SUSAN. If you're both quite sure you want me.

JANE. Want you? (*She gestures with the cake knife*) If you don't come I'll commit hara-kiri.

(CAXTON *crosses to* L *and picks up his bag*)

CATHERINE. You're a blessing in an unusually pleasant disguise.

ROSE. Hear, hear! One can do with a bit of help when one's well over eighty.

(CAXTON *crosses down* R, *puts down his bag, opens it, takes out some rag and starts to pack the vases*)

JANE (*to Susan*) Will you be bringing a TV set, by any chance?

SUSAN. I'm afraid not.

JANE. Pity. We haven't one, either, and I ought to watch how the others do it. (*She helps Caxton to pack the vases*)

CAXTON. You very easily could have one.

(CATHERINE *picks up the rubber plant and hands it to Rose*)

There are several things here I wouldn't mind giving you a very fair price on.

CATHERINE (*to change the subject; to Rose*) You've only brought three cups, Rose. We're five.

SUSAN (*moving* R *of the sofa*) Rose is kindly going to give me a cup from her pot.

PHILIP (*moving to* R *of Susan*) Mr Caxton can have mine. (*He unthinkingly puts his arm around Susan*)

(CATHERINE *stares at Philip's arm*)

I want to make sure Mrs Dawson realizes—(*he sees Catherine looking at his arm and disengages. Lamely*) realizes what she's letting herself in for. I'll have a cup with Rose, too.

ROSE. I might as well open a cafe, and have done with it.

(ROSE *stalks out, leaving the door open*)

JANE (*to Susan*) Take no notice, dear. You've caught us on an odd day. We're the most normal household really. (*She picks up her handbag*

(PHILIP *picks up the onions and crosses to the door*)

SUSAN (*following Philip to the door*) If that's true, I shall be most disappointed.

(CAXTON *completes his packing, takes out his wallet and counts some notes.* JANE *stands anxiously beside him, with her open handbag*)

CATHERINE. When you can escape from Rose, come back and we'll make all arrangements.

SUSAN. Thank you.

(PHILIP *and* SUSAN *exit, closing the door behind them.* CAXTON *replaces the notes in the wallet, puts the wallet in his pocket, bends over and examines the desk.* JANE *tosses her handbag on the stool*)

JANE (*declaiming*)

"Oh, let no noble . . ."

CATHERINE. Tea, Jane.

JANE. No, not for a minute—I must practise. (*She declaims*)
"Oh, let no noble eye profane a tear,
If I be gored by Mowbray's spear . . ."

(*She unintentionally smacks Caxton on his seat*)

(CAXTON *straightens and turns*)

Oh, Mr Caxton! I'm so sorry, I'd slightly forgotten you. Come and have a cup of tea. (*She transfers her handbag from the stool to the desk, crosses and sits* R *of Catherine on the sofa*)

(CAXTON *picks up the stool, sets it* R *of the table* LC *and sits*)

CAXTON. Ta. Just a quick one, dear—Mrs Hayling. (*He takes out his wallet and extracts thirty pounds in notes*) You'll excuse cash, eh? (*He winks*) No tax.

JANE. We prefer it. We pay everything in notes.

CATHERINE. When we have any.

JANE. The bank's so curious.

CAXTON. You're ladies after my own heart. There you are. (*He slaps the notes down on the table*) Thirty smackers.

CATHERINE. Thirty?

CAXTON (*blandly*) That's right.

JANE. I thought we'd gone higher than thirty smackers.

CAXTON. Oh, come now, dear—Mrs Hayling. You've got enough out of me without squeezing me. (*He rises quickly and moves to the desk*) It's thirty or I take it back.

JANE. Take it back! (*She quickly hides the notes in the muffin dish*)

CAXTON. And don't forget I pay top prices if you have anything else you want to get rid of.

CATHERINE. We haven't.

CAXTON. You're a bit crowded in here. How about nice summer dresses instead of, say—(*he points to the desk*) that?

JANE. We'd go about without dresses before we'd sell that.

CAXTON. I'll give you more than you expect.

CATHERINE (*firmly*) Nothing here is for sale, Mr Caxton.

CAXTON. Any old junk in the attic?

JANE. It all went as wedding presents, years ago. Tea, Mr Caxton?

(CAXTON *moves to the stool, sits and takes the cup of tea from Jane*)

Sugar?

CAXTON. Ta. (*He takes four lumps of sugar*)

JANE. Have another.

CAXTON. Ta. (*He takes another lump of sugar*) I'm interested in all types of stuff: furniture, pictures, papier mâché, glass, china, jewellery . . .

JANE (*to Catherine*) Pity I left the emeralds with the Pole.

CAXTON (*quickly*) Emeralds?

JANE. Left to us as a reward for what we endured as our husband's wives.

CATHERINE. They'd be of no interest to you.

CAXTON (*craftily*) You never know. Let me have a squint at them, eh?

JANE. Not even a sideway glance; we haven't got them here. Sandwich or chocolate biscuit?

CAXTON. Now, come on, don't give me that.

JANE (*handing cake to Caxton*) You'd prefer cake?

CAXTON. I'd prefer to have a look at your emeralds.

CATHERINE. There's no point, Mr Caxton. We're not thinking of disposing of them now.

CAXTON (*pouncing*) Now, eh? That means you were thinking of disposing of them?

JANE. When we thought they were worth two or three thousand pounds.

CAXTON (*trying not to be impressed*) Two or three thousand, eh?

CATHERINE. But we've had them valued, and it seems they're not.

CAXTON. Some people might say they were worthless hoping to get them at less than their price. You've seen what good money I pay for worthless rubbish: I pay corresponding for the real stuff.

CATHERINE. Rubbish or real, they're not for sale.

(CAXTON *sips his tea, and thinks, while gazing slyly round the room*)

CAXTON. I don't want to seem persistent, but if you ever do want to get rid of them—(*wheedlingly*) let me have first chance, eh?

CATHERINE. You're wasting your time.

CAXTON (*accusingly*) You mean you don't trust me, eh?

JANE. Don't be silly, Mr Caxton.

CAXTON (*accusingly*) You'd rather take them to one of those posh Bond Street places. Don't imagine they're beyond a little hanky-panky. You'd be far safer off with me who you know. (*He reaches over for the teapot and helps himself to tea*)

JANE. You whom we're beginning to know. (*She moves the sugar out of Caxton's reach*)

CAXTON. I can afford to give better prices: I haven't their over. heads. Go on, say you'll give me first refusal, eh?

CATHERINE. A refusal to discuss it any more is what we give.

CAXTON. Ah! (*He waves his teaspoon at Jane*) You don't trust me, I can see.

JANE (*relieving Caxton of his teaspoon*) Don't be silly, Mr Caxton.

CAXTON. Now, I want to be absolutely honest with you, so I'll tell you what I'll do.

JANE (*to Catherine; conversationally*) Catherine, remind me to tell you about the extraordinary dog I saw in Sloane Street . . .

(CAXTON *takes out his wallet and counts out one hundred pounds in notes*)

(*She rises. To Caxton*) Don't you understand short, simple phrases? (*Distinctly*) The emeralds are not for sale. *Les bijoux ne sont pas à vendre.*

CAXTON. You may change your minds.

JANE. *Jamais!* (*She resumes her seat*)

CAXTON. You have once already; therefore, it's on the cards you will again. If you do, I mean to be the buyer. And so that you'll feel safe: there you are. (*He presses the notes into Jane's hand*)

JANE. What's this?

CAXTON. A little present. To do with as you like. But which can come off the purchase price later if you want.

JANE. But the emeralds may not be worth even as much as that.

CAXTON. Then I'm the silly sausage, aren't I? (*He looks at his watch*) Christopher! It's later than I thought. (*He rises, takes his business card from his wallet and puts it on the table*) If I don't rush I'll miss a Minton dinner service. (*He picks up his bag*)

JANE. No, don't rush yet, Mr Caxton.

CAXTON (*moving up* R *of the sofa*) On that card is my telephone number. When you want more crisp notes instead of old-fashioned gems, give me a blow. (*He crosses to the door*)

CATHERINE. But this money, Mr Caxton . . .

CAXTON. Is yours to have a lovely splash about with.

JANE (*rising and moving* C) But, Mr Caxton . . .

CAXTON (*bowing*) Ladies.

(CAXTON *beams at them and exits, closing the door behind him.* JANE *gazes at the money*)

CATHERINE. How much is it?

JANE (*handing half the notes to Catherine*) Count. (*She sits* R *of Catherine on the sofa*)

(*They count frantically*)

Fifty!

CATHERINE. Fifty!

JANE (*awed*) A hundred pounds!

CATHERINE. A hundred pounds. For varnished beryls.

JANE. It's amazing.

CATHERINE. It's terrible.

JANE (*rising and moving* C) It's wonderful!

CATHERINE. But it doesn't belong to us.

JANE. He gave it to us.

CATHERINE. It is tempting.

JANE. Let's be tempted. (*She sits on the stool and imitates Caxton*) Eh, dear—Mrs Hayling?

CATHERINE (*shaking her head*) We must think more about it first.

JANE (*rising and collecting the money from Catherine*) Oh, don't be so cautious. Opportunities come once in a blue moon: they must be seized. (*She moves behind the desk and sits at it*) I've got some registered envelopes; we can just catch the evening post. This will keep the bailiffs at bay for weeks.

CATHERINE (*rising and crossing to* L *of the desk*) The worm bill's a hundred and *five*. You'll have to add five pounds of the vase money.

JANE. The vase money! I'd forgotten it. How lovely! Where is it? I gave it to you.

CATHERINE. No, you didn't.

JANE. Yes, I did.

CATHERINE. You didn't.

JANE (*rising and crossing below Catherine to the sofa*) Of course I did. I distinctly remember—I was sitting here, you were sitting there, he was over there—he gave me the money and I—put it in the muffin dish. I remember distinctly. (*She takes the notes from the muffin dish, crosses and sits at the desk*) A hundred and five for the worm-people. (*She adds five pounds to the hundred, takes a registered envelope from the drawer, and addresses it*)

CATHERINE. The remainder had better go towards light and telephone.

JANE. What about my blanket?

CATHERINE (*crossing to the bureau to get a sheaf of bills*) There won't be any current to run it if we don't settle with the Electricity Board.

JANE. Damn! Oh, well. (*She puts ten pounds in the desk drawer*) Five to electric, and five to telephone. That'll keep them quiet for a bit. I'll go round and pay them first thing. (*Sadly*) I suppose we'd better settle the next worst while we're at it. See who it is.

CATHERINE (*moving to* R *of the desk*) There's no doubt; the income tax. They've underlined "Recovery by Distraint with Costs" in red ink.

JANE. How I hate red ink! I suppose the remaining fifteen would show willing. I'll do it quickly before we think of the waste. (*She takes another registered envelope from the drawer and addresses it*) How many m's in commissioners?

CATHERINE. Two, and three s's.

JANE. Could they sue me if I put "Bloodsuckers of Inland Revenue"?

CATHERINE (*looking through the bills*) Wait a moment! The dentist hasn't had anything for ages.

JANE. Oh, we must pay him. He's a dear. Besides, Rose says she has to go again. Oh, well, there's nothing the tax people can cut off; they can go on waiting. (*She takes another envelope*) What's his address?

CATHERINE (*putting a bill on the desk*) The cleaners have been owed even longer.

JANE (*tearing up the bill and throwing it over her shoulder*) I'm not sending them anything; they demand too often.

CATHERINE. Oh, it'd better be the coal people. "No further delivery till settlement."

JANE. If I can't have an electric blanket I'm certainly having a hot-water bottle. The poor dentist must wait. (*She takes another envelope*) What's coal's address?

(ROSE *enters, leaving the door open*)

ROSE. You never rang to say you'd finished tea.

CATHERINE. You said you'd leave if we used the bell.

ROSE (*crossing to the desk*) Now we've Mrs Dawson you can again. We might as well pretend we know what's what.

JANE. Is she still here?

ROSE. Yes. Master Philip's showing her the rooms all over again. (*She cackles*) He's like a dog with two tails. I sense something in the air there.

CATHERINE (*sharply*) What do you mean?

ROSE. He has the same glint in his eye that his father had when he was gathering another into his harem. (*She crosses to the table and stacks the tea-things*)

JANE. You'll gather your cards if you're not careful. (*She puts the one hundred and five pounds into a registered envelope and seals it*) Here— pop over to the post office and register this letter. (*She picks up a pencil, rises and crosses to* R *of Rose*) The fresh air may fumigate some of your evil thoughts.

CATHERINE. But we haven't decided on the others yet.

JANE. Let's settle the bailiffs by this post, anyhow. Here you are, Rose. (*She holds out the envelope to Rose*)

ROSE (*taking no notice; intent on clearing*) I haven't reached years of maturity without knowing a glint in the eye when I see it.

JANE. Then you should recognize the murderous glint in mine. (*She takes Rose's hand and marks it with the pencil*) You're going to the "P.O." Clear? (*She slaps the envelope into Rose's hand*) Out!

(ROSE *picks up the cake-stand and exits, looking at her hand. She closes the door*)

(*She moves up* C) If she wasn't a hundred and one we ought to sack her.

CATHERINE (*replacing the bills in the bureau; worried*) She's a canny old bird, though. And has a sixth sense where sex is concerned. She knew what Basil was going to do before he made the first overtures.

JANE. But this Mrs Dawson isn't at all Philip's type. He's always gone in for exotic flamboyant creatures, like that extraordinary Fiona whatever her name is.

CATHERINE. Fiona Renshaw. (*She sits in the armchair down* R) Yes; though with Fiona I think it's a case of the hunter being hunted.

(PHILIP *enters carrying a dressmaker's dummy*)

PHILIP. This undressed female was lying abandonedly on Mrs Dawson's bed.

JANE (*moving to* L *of the desk*) Basil's mother. I thought we'd got rid of her years ago.

PHILIP. Well, will you now? (*He leaves the door open and puts the dummy on the chair below the door*)

CATHERINE. There's something we really can sell to Mr Caxton.

PHILIP (*crossing to* C) You can't. (*Firmly*) You're not to have anything more to do with Mr Caxton.

JANE. Why not?

PHILIP. Because he's a sharp, cunning old rascal.

JANE. He paid well for those ghastly vases.

PHILIP. He offered half first. (*He sits on the sofa and helps himself to a muffin*) And I'd have got double if you'd have let me.

JANE (*moving up* R *of the table*) Do you think so?

PHILIP. I know so. These dealers are menaces. They're so mad for goods they'll do anything to get them. Now that he's seen what's here, you'll have to be very careful.

CATHERINE (*rising and moving to* R *of Jane; worried*) What do you mean?

PHILIP. Look at the way he drooled over the furniture. He'll stop at nothing to get it in his clutches.

CATHERINE. But we told him it wasn't for sale.

PHILIP. That won't put him off.

JANE (*also getting worried*) What could he do?

PHILIP. Well, you're not exactly business-women. He could try and place you under some obligation.

JANE (*suddenly realizing*) Obligation!

CATHERINE. Obligation?

PHILIP. Entangle you with some little ruse, so that you're forced into doing business.

JANE
CATHERINE } (*together*) We wouldn't be.

PHILIP. You wouldn't realize till too late. (*He rises and moves to* L *of Jane*) Take my advice for once, and don't let him in the house again. (*Seriously*) Otherwise, tied up or not tied up, you'll be stripped of the furniture, and prosecuted by the trustees. (*He crosses to the door and picks up the dummy*) It's the attic for you, my love. (*To Jane and Catherine*) I'm warning you.

(PHILIP *exits with the dummy, closing the door behind him*)

CATHERINE (*alarmed*) Jane!

JANE. It's all right. (*Doubtfully*) I hope.

CATHERINE. It's not! Caxton was "entangling" us. I knew it was extraordinary to give us money without seeing the emeralds.

JANE (*crossing below Catherine and standing down* R) Now, don't always see the bad grape on the bunch first.

CATHERINE. But I suddenly realize; he doesn't care whether the emeralds are good or not.

JANE. Of course he does!

CATHERINE. I suppose he *hopes* they are. But Philip's right: his main object was to have us owing him money.

JANE. So that we're forced to stock his shop. The fiend! (*She thinks for a moment then moves to* L *of the desk. Brightly*) We'll send his money back again.

CATHERINE (*moving to* L *of Jane*) We can't. It's on its way to the worm people.

JANE. So it is! (*She rushes to the window*) Rose—Rose . . .

CATHERINE. She'll be at the post office by now.

JANE. Damn! (*She moves to* L *of the desk*) Well, we'll have to ring the worm people, and say we paid them by mistake.

CATHERINE. That'd mean the bailiff nightmare all over again.

JANE (*crossing down* L) Anything rather than that.

CATHERINE (*sitting on the sofa at the right end; frantically*) We must think of something. Quickly.

JANE (*sitting on the sofa at the left end*) It's no use trying to hurry my brain. It either seizes up, or goes fantastic.

(*They sit thinking*)

CATHERINE. The more I think, the worse it seems.

JANE. Don't be so pessimistic, Catherine. Think good things, and you'll attract them.

CATHERINE. You'll attract something you don't expect in a moment.

(*They continue thinking*)

JANE (*suddenly*) Of course, Caxton isn't in *need* of the money, or he wouldn't have given it to us.

CATHERINE. What is the point of that remark?

JANE (*importantly*) We'll offer to pay it back.

CATHERINE. My dear Jane . . .

JANE. Listen! He won't *accept* the offer because he'd lose his claim on the emeralds, or if they're worthless, on the furniture. But it'll calm any suspicions he may get, and give me time to get on TV and *earn* some money. (*She rises, picks up Caxton's card and crosses to the desk*) I'll ring him up straight away. (*She lifts the receiver*)

CATHERINE. Suppose he does accept your offer?

JANE. Of course he won't. I've explained . . . (*She replaces the receiver*) I suppose he just might. (*Brightly*) We must borrow a hundred pounds in case he does.

CATHERINE (*rising and moving to* L *of Jane*) We'd only have to repay that as well.

JANE. Yes, but as we'd borrowed it later, we could pay it back later. We'd just owe the person a hundred pounds instead of Caxton.

CATHERINE. What person?

(ROSE *enters, leaving the door open*)

ROSE (*moving to the table*) My admirer in the post office dealt with me in front of the whole queue. (*She cackles*) They were livid. (*She stacks the tea-things*)

JANE (*to Catherine; sotto voce*) Do you think . . . ? (*She gestures towards Rose*)

CATHERINE. You could try. (*She crosses up* L *of the sofa*)

JANE (*crossing to* R *of Rose*) Rose, dear. (*She pauses*) Rose, dear.

(ROSE *takes no notice*)

Rose! I'm talking to you.

ROSE (*replacing the stool below the desk*) I didn't think "Rose-dear" meant me.

JANE (*following Rose*) Of course it means you.

CATHERINE. You're very dear to us.

ROSE (*crossing to the table*) Pity you don't show it more.

JANE (*moving to* R *of Rose*) If we didn't love you we shouldn't treat you as we do.

ROSE. I meant by paying my wages more often.

JANE (*innocently*) Are we behindhand?

ROSE. A hundred and eight pounds twelve shillings behindhand. Haven't had anything for eleven months.

CATHERINE. You don't need it: you're rich.

ROSE. Whooh!

JANE. How much exactly have you in the post office?

ROSE. Eighty-one pounds.

JANE (*to Catherine*) Not quite enough.

ROSE. Not nearly enough after sixty-five years' hard labour.

CATHERINE (*to Jane*) Still, it would help out.

JANE. Yes. Rose, dear, you wouldn't like to add it to the hundred and eight we already owe?

ROSE (*firmly*) No!

JANE. No! (*She moves down* R) I didn't think you would, some-how.

CATHERINE. We're in serious trouble, Rose.

ROSE (*picking up the laden tray*) When haven't you been? I can't help you—(*she crosses to the door*) I must start saving for my old age.

(SUSAN *appears in the doorway*)

SUSAN. I'm just off; may I say good-bye?

JANE. Oh, Mrs . . . , come in.

(SUSAN *comes into the room*)

Rose (*crossing below Susan*) A friendly word of warning, dear; they're on the borrow.

(Rose *exits.* Susan *moves* LC. Catherine *crosses to the door and closes it*)

Jane (*laughing it off*) Don't take any notice of her; she's in second childhood. It's just a wee financial crisis that's blown up.

Catherine. And threatens to flatten us.

Susan (*moving* C) But the emeralds?

Jane. Fakes.

Susan. Oh, I am sorry.

Catherine (*moving to the sofa and sitting*) They're the cause of us wanting a few pounds.

Jane (*crossing to* R *of Susan*) I suppose—*you* haven't any moneys—lying idle?

Susan (*shaking her head*) I'm in terrible difficulties myself.

Catherine. Oh, you poor thing.

Susan. I owe for the storage of my furniture. I'm frightened they'll sell it if I don't pay soon.

Jane. Can't your husband help?

Susan (*hesitantly*) He's in America. We're divorced.

Jane (*thoughtfully*) So Rose was right—you *are* free to enter a harem.

Susan (*amazed*) I beg your pardon?

Catherine (*hastily*) We just didn't realize you were divorced.

Susan (*moving to* R *of Catherine*) I suppose I should have told you. But I was so afraid it might make a difference.

Catherine. Hardly, my dear. I went through the divorce court myself, with Basil.

Jane. I would have, but pneumonia worked faster than the lawyers.

Catherine. Divorce and debt have our fullest sympathy. How much is the storage demanding?

Susan. Just on fifteen pounds.

Jane. But that's a bagatelle!

Catherine. Compared with the hundred we need for our salvation.

Susan. A very worrying bagatelle.

Jane (*joyfully*) The vase money!

Catherine. Oh, yes.

Jane (*moving and sitting at the desk*) We'll lend you that.

Susan (*crossing to* L *of the desk*) I wouldn't hear of such a thing.

Catherine. It's an excellent idea.

Susan. I couldn't accept it, really.

Jane (*checking the notes*) Five for light—five for telephone—we have exactly fifteen left. It'll do you beautifully, and it's no good to us without the rest. (*She rises and crosses with the notes to Susan*)

Susan. No, please.

Catherine. My dear, you'll be doing us a service. If you have it Jane can't spend it.

SUSAN. This is terribly awkward . . .
JANE (*putting the notes into Susan's hand*) Don't be silly.
SUSAN. But you see—there's something you ought to know . .

(PHILIP *pops his head round the door*)

PHILIP (*in a frantic whisper*) Don't tell her I'm in whatever happens.
CATHERINE. Who?
PHILIP. You don't know where I am, or anything about me.

(PHILIP *withdraws his head.* JANE *crosses below Susan to look after Philip*)

JANE (*turning to Susan*) Are other people's houses like this? (*She crosses and stands below the desk*)
CATHERINE. Someone he knows; can't be a bailiff.

(ROSE *enters and stands above the open doorway*)

ROSE (*in a whisper*) I don't wonder Master Philip scuttled. (*She announces*) Miss . . . Now I've forgotten.

(FIONA RENSHAW *enters. She is a very lovely girl, but dressed expensively at the height of the latest absurd fashion. Her manner and speech match the extravagance of her dress*)

FIONA (*crossing to* C) Fiona Renshaw.
ROSE (*moving to* L *of Fiona*) Sorry, miss. But I'm getting on for eighty-five. I forget a bit.
FIONA. Good heav; I forget at twenty-five. After sixty more glorious years Allah knows the state my mind'll be in. Or my bod for that matter.

(ROSE, *overcome with cackling, exits, closing the door behind her. There is an awkward pause during which* JANE *moves to* R *of Fiona, goes round her up* C *and comes down* L *of her, staring all the time in silence*)

I adore being stared at, but there is a limit.
JANE. My dear, we were struck dumb by your great courage. Do sit down—oh, no, perhaps that would be a mistake. (*She moves above the left end of the sofa*)
FIONA (*gazing at her dress*) François really has exceeded his silly self, hasn't he? I've come to see Phil. Is he about?
CATHERINE. I'm—er, not sure.
FIONA. If someone went to find out would it disorg everything?
SUSAN (*crossing to the door*) I'll go, Mrs Hayling.
FIONA. Ange! Tell him I can literally only stay two mo's.
SUSAN (*with only a hint of mockery*) Then I'd better hurry.

(SUSAN *exits quickly, closing the door*)

FIONA. I'm *en route* to the airport. I simply must chase hotter sun.
JANE (*moving to* L *of the sofa*) Where are you hoping to catch it?
FIONA. Portugal.

CATHERINE. Portugal. How lovely!

FIONA. It should be—except that I'm suffering from an uneasy conch.

JANE. Try milk of magneshe.

FIONA. Have I reason to be uneasy about Phil?

CATHERINE. Why should you be?

FIONA. Well, about three weeks ago I suggested that we should tie the nuptial knot.

JANE (*sitting on the sofa* L *of Catherine*) Legally?

FIONA (*nodding*) With white sat and orange blos. He didn't seem anti, so I had illusions. Since then I've seen him twice; once in a lift, the button of which was pressed as I got there; and the second time at a dance where he disappeared into the "gents" for the rest of the eve.

JANE. He inherits it from his father.

CATHERINE. What precisely are you trying to find out?

FIONA (*moving to* L *of the desk*) As you've lived with him for twenty-five years, I thought you might know whether there's any chance of *me* now doing so?

CATHERINE. My dear, in each of those twenty-five my son's become more unpredictable.

FIONA. Oh. (*She pauses and gazes speculatively at them*) Of course, I hate to toot my own trump. But I should bring much to the match.

CATHERINE. That we can see.

FIONA. Including mun . . .

JANE. Mun? Mun? Oh, *mun!* (*She rises and crosses quickly to* L *of Fiona. Casually*) Much mun?

FIONA. The Chancellor of the Excheque thinks we're worth worrying about.

CATHERINE. We?

FIONA. Daddy. Practically port-poisoned. The estates have to come to me.

JANE. Estates? (*To Catherine*) An heiress!

FIONA. Scotland and the Bahamas.

JANE. The Bahamas. I shall get vaccinated tomorrow.

FIONA. Look, I've been frank with you because Phil's exactly what I want. Will you be dit?

JANE. Dit?

FIONA (*explaining*) O. Ditt-o.

JANE. Oh.

CATHERINE (*rising and moving to* L *of Jane*) I expect he's only avoided you because of financial difficulties. If he marries before he's thirty . . .

JANE. He loses his father's mun.

FIONA. That's Gospel, then?

JANE. Unfortunately.

CATHERINE. Basil was cranky about people not knowing their minds before they were thirty.

JANE. Something to do with marrying us before he was thirty.

FIONA (*crossing to* L *of the bureau*) But that's stupend! You send me to Portugal a happier girl.

CATHERINE. I'm glad.

FIONA. You'd approve? (*She throws open her coat and reveals a very outrageously fashionable dress*)

(JANE *takes a pair of dark glasses from the desk, puts them on, then goes to the window and closes the curtains*)

CATHERINE. Well . . .

JANE (*moving to* L *of the desk*) We'd approve of a cannibal if she had a cheque-book.

FIONA. Cheque-book! Thank you. (*She moves to* R *of the desk and takes a cheque-book from her handbag*) My excuse for coming here was to pay Phil a detteroo.

(JANE *and* CATHERINE *stare in astonishment at Fiona.*
ROSE *enters*)

ROSE. Mrs Dawson says she's gone. Master Philip's nowhere. (*She turns to go*)

FIONA (*to Jane and Catherine*) Never mind. (*She sits on the desk*)

(ROSE *pauses in the doorway*)

Now you know the situashe you can probably do more for me than I could for myself.

CATHERINE (*moving above the right end of the sofa; quickly*) We can't promise anything.

ROSE (*crossing to Jane and handing her a registered receipt*) I forgot to give you the receipt for your registered letter. You owe me three-pence. Eleven months' wages, and threepence.

(ROSE *crosses and exits, closing the door behind her.* JANE *glances at the receipt and screams involuntarily*)

CATHERINE. What is it?

JANE (*obviously shaken*) Nothing. Just practising my elocution. (*She wanders to the window*)

CATHERINE (*moving* C; *amazed*) Did I imagine it, or did you say you owed Philip money?

FIONA. Have for months. Always forget.

JANE. How much? (*She moves up* L *of the desk. Hopefully*) Not a hundred pounds?

FIONA (*shaking her head*) Just five.

JANE (*despondently*) Oh!

FIONA (*rising*) Why? Is he short of a hundred?

JANE. No; we are.

CATHERINE (*moving to* L *of Jane; quickly*) Take no notice of her. She's—(*she shakes her head at Jane*) speculating unwisely.

FIONA (*to Jane*) You poor duck; no wonder you're short. I'm always doing dit. My stockbroker has babes. Tin's my downfall. What's yours?

JANE. Emeralds.

FIONA. They'll go up again; they always do. Shall I lend you a hundred till they do?

JANE (*moving to the desk chair*) Could you? That would be kind.

CATHERINE (*horrified*) No, no!

JANE (*adamant*) Yes, yes!

FIONA (*to Catherine*) My dear, it wouldn't impov me.

JANE. But it would save our bake.

CATHERINE. Take no notice of her: she's talking dangerous nonsense.

FIONA (*filling in a cheque*) I love to hear it. Safe sense is so drear.

CATHERINE (*moving up R of the sofa*) You wouldn't think so if you were in our situation.

JANE (*moving to L of the desk*) Waiting to be thrown into pris.

FIONA (*with an exaggerated scream*) Heav! Look at the time. I must flee. I shall miss Porchers. (*She hands the cheque to Jane*) Give this to Phil—with as warm a message as you think he'll take. Any report of reciprocal emotion will find me at Poste Restante, Estoril. (*She crosses to* C)

JANE (*moving to R of Fiona*) Estoril.

CATHERINE (*moving to L of Fiona*) Please don't expect anything.

FIONA. You'll see I've made the little dear payable to *Mrs* Hayling.

JANE. Mrs Hayling—why?

FIONA. Because I've added the hundred pounds you owe your stockbroker.

CATHERINE. We refuse to take it.

FIONA (*with a naughty smile to Catherine*) And to impress upon you what a good dau-in-law I'd be, I've added another little hundred so that the first won't be lonely.

CATHERINE. No, no!

JANE. Yes, yes!

(CATHERINE *backs a little up* C)

FIONA (*crossing to the door*) I know what it is tᴜ be lonely. (*She turns. With another wicked smile*) But not for much longer, maybe. When I get back from Porchers, you must both come and have drinkies and so. *Au rev.*

(FIONA *exits, slamming the door behind her*)

JANE (*looking at the cheque and moving down* RC) Two hundred pounds!

CATHERINE (*turning on Jane and pointing her finger at her*) Procuress!

JANE. Before you use other words you'll regret: listen.

CATHERINE (*excited*) But don't you see we're "entangled" with her, too, now. (*She moves down* C) Tear it up—tear it up.

JANE. No, no. If we do it means the bailiffs for certain.

CATHERINE. The bailiffs? But we've settled the worm-people.

JANE (*moving to* R *of Catherine*) That's just it, we haven't. (*She displays the receipt*) Look at this receipt.

CATHERINE (*reading*) "Commissioners of Inland Revenue"?

JANE. I put Mr Caxton's hundred and five pounds in *their* envelope instead of the worm-people.

CATHERINE (*moving up* C; *appalled*) Jane!

JANE (*following to* R *of Catherine*) Now, keep calm, keep calm.

CATHERINE (*turning and moving down* L) But it's calamity!

JANE (*following her*) No, it isn't.

CATHERINE. It is. We've the bailiffs; Caxton owed a hundred and about to seize our furniture, which we're not allowed to sell; and Fiona about to seize Philip—(*she crosses below Jane to the desk*) who'll murder us if he finds out what we've done.

JANE (*moving* L *of the sofa and gaily waving the cheque*) But we have a cheque for two hundred pounds.

(*The standard lamp suddenly goes out*)

CATHERINE. Oh! (*She goes to the standard lamp and tries the switch. Wailing*) And now the electricity cut off.

(JANE *crosses to the door and tries to switch on the chandelier, without success*)

JANE. Splendid! (*She crosses and stands above the desk*) It means we needn't pay them anything. (*She takes five pounds from the desk drawer*) Two hundred and *five* pounds.

CATHERINE. Basil always said you weren't normal.

(JANE *lifts the telephone receiver, listens for a moment, then takes the remaining five pounds from the drawer*)

JANE. Two hundred and *ten* pounds. (*She crosses towards the door*) Come on, we'll have dinner at the *Savoy*.

CATHERINE. You're mad! Stark staring mad!

JANE (*joyously*) We've two hundred and ten lovely pounds. (*She moves* C) If we can't put our house in order with that—then let it topple about our ears.

(*The large mirror* L *crashes to the floor, smashing its glass.* JANE *and* CATHERINE *stare at the mirror as*—

the CURTAIN *falls*

ACT II

SCENE—*The same. A few days later. Seven o'clock in the evening.*

There is some rearrangement of the furniture. The sofa is now C, *facing down* L. *The armchair down* R *is now down* L *with the table from* LC *now R of the armchair. The upright chair* R *has been removed and at the downstage end of the window there is a nest of three small tables. The stool is down* R. *A small mirror is on the wall down* L, *replacing the broken one.*

When the CURTAIN *rises, the window curtains are closed and the lights are on.* CATHERINE, *in a housecoat, is* C, *carrying one of the small tables.* PHILIP, *in a dressing-gown is down* L, *repairing an electric fire. His tools, etc., are on the table down* L.

CATHERINE (*anxiously*) Are you going to be able to make it work? (*She places the small table* L *of the upright chair* L)

PHILIP. Yes; stop fussing.

CATHERINE (*crossing to the nest of tables up* R) It's amazing how everything saves itself up to go wrong till one gives an important party. (*She picks up a small table*)

PHILIP. You'll go white overnight if you worry so much.

CATHERINE (*moving and placing the table below the sofa*) But it's essential that everything goes smoothly this evening. There's much more chance of Jane getting on the television if James Blair feels under an obligation. (*She crosses to the door and calls*) Rose. Do hurry!

PHILIP. If we've got to bribe him to employ Jane, why go through all this? Why not just send him a couple of bottles of whisky?

CATHERINE (*collecting a box of fifty cigarettes from the table down* L) We can't afford a couple of bottles of whisky. (*She moves* LC)

(ROSE *enters, carrying a tray with three saucers and four small cups. During the following lines,* CATHERINE *sets out the saucers as ashtrays, puts cigarettes in the cups and sets them alongside the saucers on the small tables*)

ROSE (*as she enters*) As I was telling you—(*she crosses to* R *of Catherine*) to start with oysters, half a dozen for the ladies and a dozen for the gentlemen.

CATHERINE (*taking a saucer*) The flowered one. (*She puts the flowered saucer and a cup of cigarettes on the table* L *of the upright chair* L)

(JANE *enters and crosses to* R *of the desk. She wears an evening dress. She practices her voice production while the others, taking no notice, go on speaking*)

JANE (*emphasizing vowels*) "Mowbray's spear. Mowbray's spear. Mowbray's spear.
Oh, let no noble eye profane a tear
If I be gored by Mowbray's spear."

ROSE. Consommé—took a week to make, oodles of sherry in it, and three eggs to clear it.

CATHERINE (*crossing to the small table below the sofa*) The cracked one. (*She takes the cracked saucer from Rose's tray and puts it with a cup of cigarettes on the table below the sofa*)

ROSE. Broiled salmon with tartare sauce.

(CATHERINE *takes a cup from the tray, fills it with cigarettes, crosses and puts it on the desk*)

(*She follows to* L *of the desk*) Iced asparagus with whipped cream.

JANE (*trying again*)
    "Oh, let no noble eye profane a tear,
    If I be gored by Mowbray's spear."

(*The others take no notice*)

ROSE. Ham soufflés with sliced pickled peaches ...

JANE (*shouting*) If you three are representative of TV audiences, I've been fooling myself.

(CATHERINE *takes the last cup and saucer from the tray, fills the cup with cigarettes and puts them on the small table up* R)

PHILIP. At the moment, electricity is more important than elocution.

JANE (*crossing to* LC) You're right. Do hurry. We're never going to be ready in time.

PHILIP. Of course you are. You've a good hour before the Blairs are due.

JANE. Yes, but we're expecting Caxton at any moment.

PHILIP (*amazed*) Caxton! You can't have asked him to dinner.

JANE. Of course not.

ROSE. A joint; best end of lamb, turned upside down, with an olive stuck on each cutlet-end, like a crown.

JANE. Do hurry, Philip.

ROSE. Fresh raspberry mousse, sprinkled with chopped almonds.

CATHERINE (*crossing to the door*) Now, the nuts and olives.

(CATHERINE *exits*)

ROSE (*crossing to the door*) Croutes of finnan haddock marinated overnight, with white sauce, tarragon flavoured . . .

(ROSE *exits*)

PHILIP. I thought we were supposed to be broke?

JANE. That isn't what we're having tonight! She's just trying to make the goulash sound mean. Have you finished?

(CATHERINE *enters, carrying a table-lighter*)

PHILIP. I want some insulating tape.

CATHERINE (*crossing to the desk*) There's some in the Oxo tin on my desk.

(PHILIP *exits quickly*)

(*She puts the lighter on the desk*) I'm exhausted before we've even started. (*Sitting on the stove*) I'm sure something's going to go wrong.

JANE. Now, don't start that again.

CATHERINE. Haven't we reason to be anxious?

JANE. No. Our situation's wonderfully improved. (*She crosses to* L *of Catherine*) Everything's under control. Couldn't be better.

CATHERINE (*impatiently*) Jane, for goodness' sake stop living in this fool's paradise.

JANE. Why, if I have a lovely time there?

CATHERINE. Because you're very soon going to be turned out of it by a bailiff brandishing a flaming writ.

JANE. Nonsense! With Fiona's two hundred we've paid off the worm people, and we're about to pay off Caxton. And everyone else dangerous has enough to keep them quiet for the time being.

CATHERINE. Fiona's not going to keep quiet about her two hundred.

JANE. She's safely in Portugal.

CATHERINE. She won't stay in Portugal.

JANE. We can easily keep Philip terrified of her till I've paid her back with my TV salary. Though little Jamie will never employ me if I look haggard. (*She sits on the sofa and lies back*) Do let's be calm and relaxed. Think of rippling water.

CATHERINE. Having hooked us so satisfactorily, Caxton may not want us to escape. (*She is suddenly newly worried*) Suppose he refuses to take back the money?

JANE (*giving herself a facial*) Then we tell him about your brother in Scotland Yard.

CATHERINE. What brother? Oh! He seemed all right when we thought him up, but it doesn't sound very plausible now.

JANE. Don't worry. I can always think of something.

CATHERINE. Yes, but will it be a plausible something?

JANE. Of course.

CATHERINE. I don't trust that grasshopper mind of yours. Promise me that you won't invent anything rash.

JANE. I promise.

CATHERINE. Supposing Caxton says, "I won't take a cheque"?

JANE (*after a moment's thought*) In that case I'll tell him the emeralds don't belong solely to us.

CATHERINE. But they do!

JANE. Well, I'll think of something else.

CATHERINE. But, Jane, Caxton's very cunning . . . (*She glances at the door*) Sshh!

(PHILIP *enters carrying a roll of insulating tape*)

PHILIP (*resuming his work on the electric fire*) What are you both looking so guilty about?

JANE. You recognized it?

PHILIP. What?

JANE. My "guilty" look. I was practising my mime. See if you recognize this one. (*She rises and takes up a "horror" pose*)

CATHERINE. Not now, not now.

PHILIP (*taping the cable*) You've both been extra peculiar these last few days.

CATHERINE. I think we've been extra charming.

PHILIP. I saw you'd had another income tax demand. Is that why?

JANE. We sent them far more than they deserved only the other day.

PHILIP. In case it is, it may ease your minds to know that I sent them a hundred for you this morning.

CATHERINE (*moving to R of Jane; aghast*) You did what?

JANE (*unable to believe it*) You sen them a hundred *pounds?*

PHILIP. You can return it if any of those dud investments turn up.

CATHERINE. Where did you get a hundred pounds?

JANE. And why on earth did you waste it on the income tax?

CATHERINE. Where did it come from, Philip?

PHILIP (*finishing his repairs*) That should make it fairly safe.

(ROSE *enters carrying a dish of olives*)

ROSE (*crossing to Catherine*) Then anchovy gondolas were very popular. Served with Admiral Ross's Indian Devil Mixture. (*She puts the dish on the desk*)

JANE (*to Philip*) Are you likely to get any more from the same source?

PHILIP. No.

JANE. Well, if you do, hand it over to us immediately.

PHILIP. I'm not mad. (*He collects his tools together*)

(SUSAN *enters and crosses to L of the sofa. She carries a vase of flowers*)

SUSAN. Here are the flowers. I'm afraid that's the best I can do.

CATHERINE (*crossing and taking the vase from Susan*) Afraid! It's beautiful. (*She puts the vase on the desk*)

PHILIP. You're a marvel, darling——

(JANE *looks sharply at Philip*)

—Mrs Dawson.

ROSE (*moving down L of the desk*) A savoury always adds relish.

PHILIP (*slightly confused; covering up*) Well, she is, isn't she? No-one else could make such a display from two old three-and-sixpenny bunches. (*He plugs the fire cable into the socket in the skirting-board down L*)

CATHERINE (*glancing at her watch*) Look at the time. I must go and dress. (*She crosses to the door*) Put the final touches to the dinner table, Rose.

(CATHERINE *exits*)

ROSE (*crossing to the door*) Then, of course, dessert—nectarines, hot-house grapes, chocolates, pineapple, candied fruits, bon-bons . . .

(ROSE *exits*)

JANE (*moving to* R *of the table* L) Chocolates! I knew we'd forget something. (*She hurries to the door*) They'll have to make do with the ones I keep for the milkman's horse.

(JANE *exits.* SUSAN *crosses to the desk* PHILIP *closes the door*)

SUSAN (*arranging the flowers in the vase*) You must be more careful. Your mother noticed that.

PHILIP (*crossing to Susan*) It's your fault: you shouldn't have come in looking so luscious. (*He gazes at her for a moment then crosses to* R) Mrs Dawson?

SUSAN. Mr Hayling?

PHILIP. Come here.

SUSAN (*moving towards him*) Yes?

PHILIP. Right close, Mrs Dawson.

SUSAN (*moving close to him*) Yes?

PHILIP. Now, kiss me.

SUSAN. No, we must be . . .

PHILIP (*taking her in his arms*) Darling.

(*They kiss*)

SUSAN (*eventually pushing him away*) Darling, they might come back any moment.

PHILIP. You know, I can't bear this much longer.

SUSAN (*a little pathetically*) Do you think it's easy for me?

PHILIP (*impulsively taking her in his arms again*) No, of course it isn't. And you're wonderful about it, bless you.

SUSAN. Couldn't we be frank with them?

PHILIP. Do you want to see them even odder than they are?

SUSAN (*sitting on the stool*) I suppose it would be disastrous.

PHILIP (*standing* R *of the stool*) Worse. But it won't be for much longer. This chap I've found is sure he can fix things.

SUSAN (*ruefully*) I should hope so, considering the amount of money he wanted in advance.

PHILIP (*putting his hand over her mouth*) Ssh! They'd murder me if they found out how I raised that money.

SUSAN. Oh, I hate all this subterfuge.

PHILIP (*kneeling beside Susan*) Darling, you know I do it only because: "Beyond all limit of what else i' the world, I love, prize, honour you."

SUSAN (*softly*) Philip.

PHILIP. What's more I've only said that once before; to a very spotty scholar on the stage of my prep school.

SUSAN (*laughing and kissing him*) Darling!

(JANE *enters with a box of chocolates and two saucers.* PHILIP *rises quickly and stands* R *of the stool*)

PHILIP. She did that in the middle of Piccadilly Circus, Mrs Dawson?

SUSAN (*catching on*) Er—yes.

PHILIP. She *must* have known him. (*To Jane*) Oh, hullo.

JANE. Hullo.

PHILIP. Everything all right?

JANE. That's what I was wondering.

(PHILIP *crosses to the fire and switches it on and off*)

PHILIP. The fire is, anyhow.

JANE. Good.

PHILIP. Would you go and get the ice, Mrs Dawson? I'll mix the drinks.

SUSAN (*rising and crossing to the door*) Yes, of course, Mr Hayling.

(PHILIP *moves towards Susan*)

JANE (*moving above the sofa*) Oh, Mr Hayling . . .

(SUSAN *exits.* PHILIP *moves to* L *of Jane*)

You might tell the other Mrs Hayling that this Mrs Hayling would like to see her. Thank you, Mr Hayling.

(PHILIP *moves to the door*)

Oh, before you go, I want a word with you. Sit down, Mr Hayling.

(PHILIP *closes the door, then sits on the sofa*)

(*She stands up* R *of the sofa*) I'm going to ask you a direct question, and I want a direct answer.

PHILIP. You're the one who by-passes awkward questions.

JANE. Are you thinking of marrying Susan?

PHILIP. No.

JANE. Do you swear that by everything you hold sacred—if there is anything you hold sacred?

PHILIP. Yes.

JANE. Look me in the eyes.

(PHILIP *turns to face Jane*)

Right in the middle.

PHILIP (*gazing at her*) I repeat: I have no intention of asking Susan to marry me. Should you be interested, I have no intention of asking Fiona, either.

JANE. I'm delighted to hear it. Because she's determined to marry you.

PHILIP (*rising; astonished*) That's not what I expected you to say. You know she's an heiress?

JANE. An heiress?

PHILIP (*leaning over the sofa towards Jane*) Didn't she tell you about Scotland and the Bahamas?

JANE (*standing to attention and saluting*) England's still best.

PHILIP. That doesn't ring true. What are you up to?

JANE. We aren't up to anything. (*She moves to the desk and puts out the chocolates*) It's going to be a very good party tonight, don't you think?

PHILIP. Yes.

JANE (*moving below the sofa; anxiously*) Have you heard from Fiona lately?

PHILIP. No.

JANE. Good.

PHILIP. Good?

JANE. Good that the weather's so nice she hasn't time to write. (*She puts a saucer of chocolates on the table* L) Oh—(*she takes a chocolate from the saucer*) the horse really must have that one.

PHILIP (*moving to* R *of Jane*) You *are* up to something.

JANE. I'm up to nothing at all. Hadn't you better go and get dressed? Brigette Blair's coming early.

PHILIP (*moving towards the door*) Then I'm going to be late.

JANE (*intercepting him*) No, Philip. (*Winningly*) We want you to be specially nice to Brigette tonight. Flatter her if you can. Her knowledge can be of great use to us.

PHILIP. Her knowledge of how to keep flu at bay?

JANE. No, of course not. Her knowledge of precious stones.

PHILIP. What's that got to do with it?

JANE (*crossing to the desk*) Remind me to tell your mother there's a smell of curry powder in the linen cupboard.

PHILIP (*moving to* L *of the sofa and leaning over towards Jane*) There's more to this dinner-party than meets the eye.

JANE (*moving to* R *of the sofa*) It's to impress James Blair so that he employs me on TV. And he might even buy one of your mother's stories.

PHILIP. What else is it for?

JANE. Oh, go and mix the drinks. (*She moves to the desk*)

PHILIP. If I didn't know that you were both basically honest, I'd be worried.

(ROSE *enters*)

ROSE. The junk-man's here.

JANE. Ssh! You're not to call him that.

PHILIP (*alarmed*) Caxton? He mustn't see me.

(PHILIP *hurriedly exits*)

JANE. Why not? (*She sees Philip has gone*) And he asked me what I was up to. (*To Rose*) What's *he* up to?

ROSE. You're all up the pole as far as I can see.

(CAXTON *enters, pushing past Rose. He carries a brief-case*)

CAXTON. I followed up as she didn't seem clear I had an appointment.

ROSE. One day you'll see something you oughtn't to.

(ROSE *exits, closing the door*)

JANE (*crossing to Caxton*) She's a fountain of humour, isn't she? How nice to see you again. Do sit down.

CAXTON (*crossing and sitting on the sofa*) Ta. My momma gave me your message.

JANE (*moving to L of Caxton*) Oh! Was that your momma I spoke to on the phone? She sounded charming—what I could understand.

CAXTON. She told me you'd phoned repeatedly. I've been in North Wales.

JANE. Business or hols?

CAXTON. Supposed business. Two old Welsh ladies got me up there on false pretences.

JANE. How scandalous!

CAXTON. I've a good mind to take action against them.

JANE (*worried*) Action?

CAXTON. It happens all the time. I chase hundreds of miles after goods, and find as much as if I'd sat on the beach with my mouth open. It makes me wild. Never mind—(*he rubs his hands*) I'm not going to have that trouble with you, eh?

JANE. I'm afraid you are, Mr Caxton.

CAXTON. Eh?

JANE (*crossing to R of the desk*) We've decided to give you back your hundred pounds as we're definitely not selling the emeralds.

CAXTON (*rising and moving up L of the desk*) Come now, dear—Mrs Hayling. I'm sure you don't mean that.

JANE. I'm sure I do. (*She picks up a cheque from the desk*) So here is your cheque all ready.

CAXTON. Now, half a jiff: don't let's be hasty.

JANE. Yes, do let's be hasty.

CAXTON. But you promised to sell them to me.

JANE. We did nothing of the sort.

CAXTON. I certainly understood you did. (*With underlying threat*) And as you've accepted my deposit, in the eyes of the law you're under an obligation to sell.

JANE. The eyes of the law didn't know they weren't worth selling. (*She holds out the cheque*) So here you are.

CAXTON (*ignoring the cheque and moving down RC*) I'm not taking a cheque.

JANE (*following Caxton*) Of course you are.

CAXTON. I'm not. I came here to buy the emeralds, and I'm going to sit here till I do. (*He crosses and sits on the sofa at the right end*)

(*There is a pause as* JANE *crosses to R of Caxton and stands looking at him. Then she makes up her mind*)

JANE. Then you're going to have a very long sit. You see—it's absolutely impossible for us to sell the emeralds because—(*after a long breath*) they don't belong solely to us.

CAXTON. What?

JANE (*happily holding out the cheque*) So you see you've got to take your cheque back.

CAXTON (*waving it aside*) Now, look. The emeralds were left jointly to the wives of the late Mr Basil Hayling, weren't they?

JANE (*uncertainly*) Er—yes.

CAXTON. Aren't you and the other Mrs Hayling the only wives?

JANE (*playing for time*) What's that?

CAXTON. I said, aren't you and the other Mrs Hayling the only wives?

JANE (*with a flash of inspiration*) No!

CAXTON. You're not going to tell me he was married a third time?

JANE (*after a moment's pause*) That's exactly what I am going to tell you. At least—wait a moment—let me think whether I should or not. (*After a moment's thought*) Yes.

CAXTON. You might as well spill everything having gone so far. There's a third Mrs Hayling, eh?

JANE. Yes, a third Mrs Hayling.

CAXTON. Why haven't we heard of her before?

JANE (*after more thought*) It's something we prefer to keep dark.

CAXTON. Why?

JANE (*confidentially*) Well, Basil didn't actually go through the marriage ceremony with her.

CAXTON. Then she's not a wife.

JANE. She was in every other way; if you know what I mean. Yes, I'm sure you know what I mean. Even changed her name to Mrs Hayling by deed poll. (*She moves above the sofa*)

CAXTON (*rising and moving below the desk; worried*) Three of you in it, eh? That's nasty—very nasty.

JANE (*moving to L of the sofa; delightedly*) Couldn't be nastier, could it?

CAXTON. Wouldn't Number Three agree to the sale? After all, you can't all wear the things.

JANE (*worried*) No, we can't, can we? (*Inspired*) But once before we suggested selling them, and Number Three turned very acid.

CAXTON (*moving to R of the sofa*) I wonder if I mightn't be able to persuade her.

JANE. I'm quite sure you wouldn't.

CAXTON. Let me go and see her and have a try.

JANE. Impossible.

CAXTON. Why?

JANE. She—lives abroad now.

CAXTON. Where?

JANE (*with only the slightest pause*) Portugal—Estoril.

CAXTON (*sitting on the sofa at the right end*) I'll pay in escudos: that might make all the difference to her.

JANE. No, it wouldn't. She's very wealthy.

CAXTON. If she's very wealthy she has no need of old-fashioned jewels.

JANE. Well, when I say she's wealthy, she isn't *herself*. She married a very rich Portuguese—a sardine manufacturer.

CAXTON. If she has no money, all the more reason for her to sell her share. She probably doesn't realize that hundreds are here just for the asking.

JANE. Oh, yes, she does. (*She sits* L *of Caxton on the sofa. After a moment's desperate thought*) I want to be absolutely honest with you, Mr Caxton.

CAXTON. That's all I ask.

JANE. Well—(*she rises and moves up* L *of the sofa*) a friend of hers came over here last summer—in July. July the fourteenth I think it was.

CAXTON. Never mind the date.

JANE (*moving above the sofa; brilliantly inventing*) And this friend raised four hundred pounds on the emeralds, from a man in the City.

CAXTON. What!

JANE (*moving to* R *of the sofa*) Thirty-four, Throgmorton Street, I think it was.

CAXTON (*horrified*) He paid up four hundred?

JANE. In cash. (*Triumphantly*) So you see, should we ever sell, we're entirely committed to this City man. So there's your cheque back. (*She holds out the cheque*)

CAXTON (*taking the cheque*) This is serious. (*Accusingly*) If you knew that you shouldn't have accepted my deposit.

JANE (*sitting on the stool*) We *didn't* know this then. We were flabbergasted this morning when we had a cable from Number Three asking us to see whether he'd put up more mun—money.

CAXTON. More.

JANE. We, of course, telephoned you immediately. But where were you? (*Accusingly*) Playing on the beach with the Welsh ladies.

CAXTON (*rising, moving and putting the cheque on the desk*) This is a serious setback. We must think what we can do.

JANE (*joyfully*) There's nothing we can do. It's fool-proof.

CAXTON (*slowly walking around Jane on the stool and finishing* R *of her*) There's a way round everything, and we must find it. You see— I want to be absolutely honest with you . . .

JANE. That's all I ask.

CAXTON. I've already got a customer interested in the emeralds. More or less promised him first refusal.

JANE (*rising, moving above the sofa and picking up Caxton's brief-case*) Well, now you'll have to unpromise it. It's out of the question. I'm a very busy woman. Good evening. (*She holds out the case*)

CAXTON. Wait a moment.

(JANE *drops the brief-case on to the sofa and moves up* L *of the sofa. All the following moves are made in a continuous walk by* JANE *trying to escape from* CAXTON *who pursues her very closely, eventually cornering her*)

(*He follows Jane*) Let me have a look at them.

JANE. What's that?

CAXTON. I want to see the emeralds.

JANE (*moving to* L *of the sofa*) You can't.

CAXTON. Why not?

JANE (*moving down* L *of the table* L) We've left them with our Polish watchmaker.

CAXTON (*moving quickly up* L *of the table* L) I'll go there, then.

JANE. You can't.

CAXTON. Why not?

JANE (*changing course and crossing down* R) I've remembered.

(CAXTON *closely follows Jane*)

He's sent them back to the strong-room at the bank. (*She moves to* R *of the desk*)

CAXTON (*moving above the desk*) It's essential I see them. You must get them out again.

JANE. I can't.

CAXTON. Why?

JANE. Each time we take them out we have to have a signed agreement from Number Three. (*She moves to* R *of the stool*)

CAXTON (*moving to* L *of the stool*) We can't waste time. (*After rapid thought*) Now, this is what we must do . . .

JANE. No, we mustn't!

(*During the next few lines* JANE *attempts to cross to* L *but each time* CAXTON *is in her way*)

CAXTON. Cable Number Three that I'll give a better price than this City chap.

JANE. But she's already had his four hundred.

CAXTON. She must pay it back again.

JANE. She can't.

CAXTON. Why not?

JANE. She's gambled it all away.

CAXTON (*advancing on Jane*) Gambled?

JANE (*retreating to the bureau*) On bullfights. (*She leans on the bureau, exhausted*)

CAXTON. You must advance it for her.

JANE (*turning on him*) We haven't any money. I mean—it's all tied up in trust.

(JANE, *after one or two more efforts to pass* CAXTON *is now really cornered*)

Don't keep following me around. (*As she cannot pass either side of the stool she walks over the stool itself, using Caxton as support, then sinks on to the sofa at the right end*) I feel I've climbed the Matterhorn.

(CAXTON *moves to* L *of the desk, takes his cheque-book from his pocket and fills in a cheque with his back to her*)

What are you doing? (*She rises and moves to* L *of Caxton*) What are you doing?

CAXTON. I must have those emeralds. (*He moves above the sofa and picks up his brief-case*) I'll pop round to my customer straight away, and explain there's been a slight hold-up.

JANE (*moving below the desk*) A complete hold-up.

CAXTON. Get Number Three to pay off the City man, and let me have the receipt.

JANE. Surely I've made it clear? She's *unable* to pay off the City man.

CAXTON. I've fixed that.

JANE. You can't have.

CAXTON. I have.

JANE. How?

CAXTON. I've left a cheque for the four hundred pounds on your desk.

(CAXTON *exits quickly, leaving the door open*)

JANE. I can't hear! I can't hear! (*She picks up the cheque and looks at it*) But I can see! (*She staggers, with exclamations to* L *and stands below the table*)

(CATHERINE *enters, having changed into an evening dress*)

CATHERINE (*closing the door*) I saw Caxton disappearing. (*She crosses to* L *of the sofa*) Have you dealt with him?

JANE. In a manner of speaking. When everything swims round does it mean one's going to faint?

CATHERINE. Jane, what's the matter?

JANE (*sinking into the armchair down* L) Could I have a cup of hot sweet tea?

CATHERINE. Don't be ridiculous! It's long past tea-time. (*She crosses to* R *of the table* L. *Suddenly suspicious*) Jane, what have you done?

JANE. Nothing, darling, nothing.

CATHERINE. Then why have you got that wild gleam in your eye?

JANE. Well, something's just happened. You may think it peculiar first hearing . . .

CATHERINE. I'll judge that. What is it?

JANE. I'll tell you when we do the washing-up tonight.

CATHERINE. You'll tell me this very minute.

JANE (*faintly*) Caxton's lent us another four hundred pounds.

CATHERINE (*after a moment's pause*) This is no time for silly jokes.

JANE. Four hundred—look. (*She hands the cheque to Catherine*)

(CATHERINE *looks at the cheque and screams*)

CATHERINE. What on earth have you done?

JANE. Keep calm, keep calm. He hasn't really lent it to *us*. He's lent it to the *other* Mrs Hayling.

CATHERINE. What other Mrs Hayling?

JANE. The one who married Basil after us. Number Three.

CATHERINE. You're mad.

JANE. Yes, I think I am, But I can't do anything about it.

CATHERINE (*moving up* R *of Jane*) We'll go into it when you're calmer. But now I'm going to tear this up.

JANE (*snatching the cheque from Catherine*) No, you're not. (*Excitedlv*) I've just thought. (*She rises*) It's our salvation.

CATHERINE. It was bad enough owing him a hundred. Five hundred and we might as well carry our belongings down to his furniture van.

JANE (*crossing to the sofa to* R *of it*) Catherine, our troubles are over. (*She hugs the cheque and explains*) Caxton's determined to lend us money. All right. We'll borrow it. Instead of paying him off, we'll pay Fiona off. That *still* leaves us with two hundred. (*Joyfully*) Two hundred. It's marvellous! We'll go to Paris for two weeks.

CATHERINE. We'll go to Holloway for two years.

JANE. Can I help it if people force money on us?

(ROSE *enters and stands above the doorway.* CATHERINE *moves down* L *of the doorway*)

ROSE. Are the windows closed?

JANE. What?

ROSE. Mrs Blair's arrived. She won't come in unless the windows are closed.

CATHERINE. They are.

ROSE (*turning and calling*) Yes, they are. (*She turns to* Jane) When I said you were up the pole I'd forgotten this one. (*She announces*) Mrs Blair.

(BRIGETTE BLAIR *enters and stands just inside the doorway. She is a strange, brusque woman without a trace of make-up, oddly dressed, with her hair in a silver-net turban. She never removes her gloves. She carries an outsize handbag.*
      ROSE *exits, closing the door*)

BRIGETTE. I'm sorry to be fussy about the windows, but draught's influenza's best friend.

(JANE *moves down* R *of Brigette and* CATHERINE *down* L *of her*)

JANE ⎱
CATHERINE ⎰ (*together*) ⎰ Brigette.
                      ⎱ How lovely to see you.

(JANE *and* CATHERINE *move to embrace Brigette*)

BRIGETTE. No, please! Kissing's asking for trouble. (*She crosses down* L *of the sofa*) The last time I was kissed I was in bed for three weeks.

JANE (*crossing down* R *of the sofa*) How very interesting! We ought'nt to kiss you, anyway. We're very peeved with you.

CATHERINE (*moving to* L *of Brigette*) You haven't been near us for ages.

BRIGETTE. London air's so full of germs that I go out as little as possible. But I do feel guilty, so here's a wee peace offering. (*She takes a parcel from under her cloak, hands it to Jane, then crosses below Catherine and stands above the table L)*

JANE *(crossing to the desk)* How exciting, thank you so much. *(She opens the parcel)*

(BRIGETTE *puts her bag on the table L and takes out a large bottle and a tissue)*

CATHERINE *(moving to R of Brigette)* What are you doing, Brigette?
BRIGETTE *(dabbing her face)* Alcohol. Everything I can't cover I disinfect.

JANE *(looking at the contents of the parcel)* Elvas plums. How delicious. *(She puts the wrapping-paper in the waste-paper basket under the desk)*
CATHERINE. Elvas plums. I adore them. How kind.

(JANE moves down R of the sofa. BRIGETTE moves above the sofa, removes her cloak and puts it over the back of the sofa)

BRIGETTE. They should be moderately hygienic because sun bakes out disease. They come from Portugal.
JANE. Portugal! How interesting. *(She moves to R of Catherine and offers her the plums)*

(BRIGETTE *throws the used tissue into the waste-paper basket)*

It's just the place we want to know about—*(to Catherine)* isn't it?
CATHERINE. Why?
JANE *(meaningly)* The woman we were talking about just now comes from there.
CATHERINE. What woman?
JANE. Number Three.

(CATHERINE *looks blank)*

Never mind—*(firmly)* but you want to know about Portugal. *(She turns to Brigette)* Have you ever been there, Brigette?
BRIGETTE *(moving down R of the sofa)* Just for a few hours when I was on a cruise with a dypsomaniac aunt.
JANE. That'll do.
BRIGETTE. But I was only there while auntie refuelled. *(She takes a silk shawl from her bag)*
JANE *(moving to L of the sofa)* Sit down and tell us all about it.
BRIGETTE *(spreading the shawl on the sofa)* You don't mind if I sit on silk?

(CATHERINE *moves and stands above the sofa)*

JANE. I don't if you don't.

(BRIGETTE *sits on the sofa.* JANE *moves the upright chair L to R of the table L, sits and eats the plums.* CATHERINE *crosses above the sofa to R of it)*

BRIGETTE. Well now, Portugal. The main thing I remember is the smell.

JANE. Nice or nasty?

BRIGETTE. Fearful. Dried fish.

JANE. Dried fish? Remember, Catherine; it may come in useful. (*To Brigette*) What else?

BRIGETTE. They have superb architecture, of course. Byzantine—wonderful stonework carved like lace.

JANE. Like lace—remember, Catherine.

BRIGETTE. But their narrow streets! Dirty and smelly, and always festooned with shawls and smalls.

CATHERINE (*sitting* R *of Brigette on the sofa*) You don't make it sound very attractive.

BRIGETTE. Well, at least it was hot. Which is more than one can say of this miserable country. No wonder flu's rampant. Do you know, I've been attacked four times this year.

JANE. You must stop going out at night.

BRIGETTE. I've had a fearful time. And appalling doctor's bills. It's really got me down. So much so that I'm bowing to the supremacy of the British germ.

JANE. What do you mean?

BRIGETTE. I'm off to the Argentine.

CATHERINE. You're going to the Argentine?

BRIGETTE. Uh, huh.

CATHERINE. For how long?

BRIGETTE. Until cremation.

CATHERINE. What about money? Aren't there regulations about taking it in and out?

BRIGETTE. The way I'm taking it out they won't know.

CATHERINE. How?

BRIGETTE. Well, I'm rather knowledgeable about precious stones . . .

JANE (*interrupting excitedly*) Oh, yes. That's why we asked you tonight. (*Hastily*) Partly why we asked you tonight.

CATHERINE. We want your advice.

BRIGETTE. Willingly. I adore jewels. It's the only excitement I have left.

CATHERINE. Can you tell us about emeralds?

BRIGETTE. Everything. What in particular?

CATHERINE. Well, suppose we had an elaborate spray of first-class Indian emeralds. What colour would they be?

BRIGETTE (*lovingly*) A gorgeous, deep, velvety, mossy green.

CATHERINE. Very descriptive.

JANE. And what sort of size?

BRIGETTE. Well, the first Shah of Persia was reported to have one as big as a hen's egg. But an ambitious bantam's egg would be nearer the truth.

JANE. And what would a string of bantam's eggs be worth?

BRIGETTE. Prices depend on whether you're buying or selling.

JANE. We're selling.

BRIGETTE (*rising; with sudden interest*) You're selling some emeralds?

CATHERINE (*quickly*) No, no. Take no notice of her.

BRIGETTE. Indeed I shall. If you're thinking of selling emeralds, I'm the very person you want.

CATHERINE. No, no, you're not.

BRIGETTE. I told you I was taking my money to the Argentine. That's how.

JANE. How?

BRIGETTE. Jewellery. With the caution of my alcoholic aunt I'm turning my capital into precious stones.

JANE. Won't the Customs object?

BRIGETTE. For some reason Customs people like to get through me quickly. Besides, there are parcels posted to oneself, friends who'll wear a piece or two; innumerable channels.

JANE. I'd be terrified. I've never got over them finding pound notes in my vanishing cream.

BRIGETTE. I have absolutely no conscience. Why shouldn't one do what one likes with one's own? My only concern is that they could trace my purchases. But a private sale such as your emeralds is ideal.

CATHERINE. We haven't any emeralds for sale, Brigette.

JANE. No, Brigette. (*She rises, leaving the plums on the table L*)

BRIGETTE. My dear girls: we get older hourly; why waste time in prevarication? If you've no emeralds why this probing?

CATHERINE. We're in a lot of trouble, Brigette . . .

JANE (*confidingly*) You see, a wretched dealer gave us a deposit thinking we meant to sell . . .

BRIGETTE (*moving above the table L; interrupting*) Who was the dealer?

CATHERINE. A Hungarian Cockney.

BRIGETTE. Not Julius Caxton?

JANE (*sitting in the armchair down L*) Correct.

BRIGETTE. I've bought from him often. Crooked as a corkscrew.

JANE. You're just trying to upset us.

BRIGETTE (*pensively*) If he's after your emeralds, they're worth being after. What did he offer you?

JANE. Well—er . . .

CATHERINE. It's all rather a muddle . . .

BRIGETTE (*moving to L of the sofa*) I'm sure. When an innocent fly walks into his parlour she's had it. (*She moves above the table L*) How much has he paid you in cash?

JANE. Five hundred pounds.

BRIGETTE. Five hundred pounds! Deposit? That means you haven't handed the emeralds over yet?

CATHERINE. No. You see . . .

BRIGETTE. He'll diddle you as sure as death. (*Business-like*) Now, what I suggest is this . . .

JANE (*rising quickly and crossing to L of the sofa; horrified*) No, no, *don't* suggest anything, please.

BRIGETTE. You must pay him off. *I'll* give you the five hundred pounds.

(JANE *sits* L *of Catherine on the sofa*)

JANE (*to Catherine; conversationally*) Shall we have cinnamon-coloured walls next time?

BRIGETTE (*taking a cheque-book and pen from her handbag*) I'll make out a cheque.

CATHERINE } (*together*) { You'll do nothing of the sort!
JANE   { No!

(BRIGETTE *moves to the sofa and tugs at her silk shawl*)

BRIGETTE (*to Jane*) Lift a minute, dear. (*She pulls out the shawl, crosses above the sofa and puts the shawl on the desk chair*) We'll go to an independent expert, and have them valued. (*She sits at the desk*)

JANE (*rising and moving above the left end of the sofa*) No, we won't.

(CATHERINE *rises and stands up* L *of the desk*)

BRIGETTE. And I'll pay you ten per cent more than he quotes as their market value. (*She fills in a cheque*) I'll gain, you'll gain; there won't be any fees or commission . . .

CATHERINE. Once and for all, Brigette, no.

BRIGETTE. I'm not listening.

JANE (*moving down* L *of Catherine; shouting*) They're probably worthless.

BRIGETTE. I can be as stubborn as a bus conductress. (*She rises and moves below the desk to* R *of Jane*) There you are. (*She holds out the cheque*) Five hundred.

CATHERINE (*retreating above the desk to* R *of it*) We refuse to accept it.

BRIGETTE. My dears . . .

JANE. If you could see them, you'd see.

BRIGETTE. Then let me see them.

CATHERINE. Unfortunately, we can't at the moment.

JANE. Even old Caxton hasn't seen them.

BRIGETTE. Is it conceivable that the old twister should give you five hundred if he hadn't set eyes on them?

CATHERINE. It may not be conceivable, but it's the truth.

PHILIP (*off; calling*) Mother!

CATHERINE (*starting violently*) Ssh! There's Philip.

BRIGETTE. Ah, he'll have more sense.

JANE (*frantically*) No, he doesn't know anything about them. And mustn't.

BRIGETTE. He will, if you don't take this in your timid hand.

JANE (*appealingly*) Brigette, remember how I saved you from that ghastly little man at the Chelsea Arts Ball.

BRIGETTE. Listen! You want to appear on TV, don't you?

JANE. I'm determined to appear on TV.

BRIGETTE (*warningly*) My boy Jamie will never employ anyone I don't approve of.

JANE (*taking the cheque from Brigette*) Well, the gypsy warned you.

(PHILIP *enters. He is now wearing a dinner jacket and carries a cocktail*)

PHILIP. Mother, see if you think . . . (*He sees Brigette*) Oh!

BRIGETTE (*crossing to* R *of Philip*) Philip, how nice to see you.

(JANE *crosses, sits at the desk and puts the cheque on it*)

(*Concerned*) Though you look flushed. Are you sure you haven't a temperature?

PHILIP (*shaking hands with Brigette*) It's the pleasure of meeting you. (*To Catherine*) Which of you will try this, and see if it's all right?

(CATHERINE *shakes her head*)

JANE. You, Brigette. Two sips of alcohol when I feel as I do, and I insult everyone.

BRIGETTE (*taking the glass*) I'll be glad to. Alcohol's a powerful disinfectant. (*She sips the drink*) It needs a little more gin. (*She returns the drink to Philip*)

JANE. A lot more gin. Little Jamie must see me through a haze.

CATHERINE. You know more about it, Brigette. Be a dear, and go and help him get it right.

BRIGETTE. If I can also cast my eye over the dinner. You ordered Rose to treat the fruit and vegetables as I told you?

CATHERINE. The meal's guaranteed germ free.

(JANE *nods frantically to* PHILIP *who acknowledges her meaning*)

PHILIP. Come and make sure, Mrs Blair.

(BRIGETTE *collects her cloak from the sofa*)

You're looking very chic this evening.

BRIGETTE (*collecting her handbag*) Don't talk balderdash! I dress against the climate, not to attract. The corsets I endured for love. (*She crosses to the desk and collects her cheque-book*) Thank God I'm too old for all that, now.

PHILIP. You're not old at all.

BRIGETTE. I am, and I'm delighted. (*She tugs at the shawl on the desk chair, extracts it and crosses to the door*) With the weather getting colder and colder every year the sooner I'm sitting by hell-fire the better.

(BRIGETTE *and* PHILIP *exit*)

CATHERINE. Jane!

JANE (*rising and moving* L *of the desk*) I know! Tear it up.

CATHERINE (*frantically*) We daren't. She'd tell Philip. Then he'd find out about Fiona, Caxton, the emeralds, everything. Jane, think of something.

JANE (*circling the stool and imitating Caxton*) Caxton says there's a way round everything. We must find it. (*Suddenly*) I know. (*She stands down* L *of the desk*) We'll blackmail Brigette.

CATHERINE. Blackmail her?

JANE. Tackle her secretly after dinner, and threaten that unless she takes her cheque back, we'll tell your brother in the Customs about her.

CATHERINE (*crossing to the bureau*) Another brother? It's too unlikely.

JANE (*sitting on the stool*) My brain's been overtaxed.

(ROSE *enters, crosses and drops a packet into Jane's lap*)

What's this?

ROSE. It was in my mattress.

JANE. This is no time to complain about lumps in your mattress.

ROSE. As I basted the chickens I felt guilty about not confessing it before. (*She crosses to the door*)

CATHERINE. What are you blathering about, Rose?

ROSE (*stopping and turning*) That's what you are, I suppose. Two plucked chickens.

JANE. She's drunk the sherry I gave her to put in the trifle.

ROSE. So you better have it.

CATHERINE. What is it?

ROSE. My secret savings: a hundred pounds.

(ROSE *exits, closing the door*)

CATHERINE (*moving to R of Jane*) Oh!

JANE (*looking at the package; musingly*) Now, does this help, or make things worse?

CATHERINE. It's amazing, but we don't really want it.

JANE. But it's very sweet of her, and we mustn't hurt her feelings. How embarrassing. (*Thoughtfully*) Perhaps having it in cash makes it rather less embarrassing. (*She opens the package*)

CATHERINE. No, Jane. (*She takes the package from Jane and puts it on the desk*)

JANE. I've got muddled as to where we are. Let's have an add! (*She checks on her fingers*) Five hundred from Brigette; four hundred from Caxton, plus the first hundred——

CATHERINE (*moving to R of Jane*) A thousand.

JANE. —two hundred from Fiona——

CATHERINE. Twelve hundred.

JANE. —the hundred we'll have to pay Philip back——

CATHERINE. Thirteen hundred.

JANE. —and a hundred from Rose.

CATHERINE. Fourteen hundred.

JANE. Fourteen hundred pounds! (*She rises and stands L of the stool*) Do you realize we could take a taxi from here to Golders Green fourteen hundred times.

CATHERINE. What's that got to do with it?

JANE. It makes you realize how much it is.

CATHERINE. I'm very well aware how much it is. And that it has to be paid back.

JANE. The point is we've got it.

CATHERINE. One thousand four hundred pounds of other people's money on one side, and a tawdry piece of bijouterie on the other.

(SUSAN *enters excitedly. She carries a tray with two cocktails on it*)

SUSAN (*moving down* L *of the sofa*) Mr Hayling was sure you'd need these.

CATHERINE. He's right.

JANE (*crossing to* R *of Susan*) Thank you.

(CATHERINE *crosses to* R *of Jane*)

(*She hands a glass to Catherine*) Here you are, dear. (*She takes a glass for herself*)

CATHERINE. They're very long ones.

SUSAN. He said you'd had a very long session with Mrs Blair.

JANE (*putting her glass on the table below the sofa*) I'd better not drink tonight.

SUSAN. But I've really burst in because I've had wonderful news.

CATHERINE. Tell us.

SUSAN. My lawyer's rung up to say he's got quite a large sum out of my ex-husband.

JANE (*moving above the right end of the sofa*) That *is* wonderful.

SUSAN. I've told him to pay the fifteen pounds you so kindly lent me into your account——

JANE. You needn't have bothered; there was no hurry.

SUSAN. —together with another eighty-five, so that you can settle your hundred-pound debt.

(SUSAN *exits quickly, closing the door*)

CATHERINE (*moving to* L *of the stool*) Fifteen hundred!

JANE. These cheques sailing in will kill our bank manager.

CATHERINE (*sitting on the stool*) They'll kill me. And you'll find "Caxton" engraved on my heart.

JANE (*moving to* L *of Catherine; suddenly*) Do I look normal?

CATHERINE. Fairly.

JANE (*searching Catherine's face*) So do you. Yet we must be completely *potty* if we're worrying about too *much* money.

(ROSE *enters and crosses to* L *of the sofa.* JANE *moves to* R *of the sofa*)

ROSE. Here's some more cash.

JANE. The bank's closed!

ROSE (*displaying a coin*) Half a crown. He gave it to me to say he's here again.

CATHERINE (*rising*) Who's here again?

ROSE. Mr Caxton. (*She moves the chair from* R *of the table* L *and puts it against the wall below the door*)

JANE. Mr Caxton! You're mad.

ROSE. Who's mad's a matter of opinion. But he's here.

CATHERINE. Send him away.

(ROSE *turns to go*)

JANE. No, wait a minute.

(ROSE *stops and turns*)

CATHERINE. Send him away, Rose

(ROSE *turns to go*)

JANE. No, Rose.

(ROSE *stops and turns*)

(*To Catherine*) It means he's seen through my story. (*She crosses to R of Rose*) Make him wait two minutes, then bring him up.

ROSE. I'm too old to understand such confusion.

(ROSE *exits, shaking her head, and closes the door*)

JANE (*thinking*) He's suspicious. We'd better switch plans again.

CATHERINE (*moving and sitting on the sofa at the right end*) I agree with Rose: I can't understand such confusion. (*She puts her drink on the table below the sofa*)

JANE (*pacing up LC*) We must keep flexible. (*She paces down LC*) That's how generals win battles—flexibility. And drink. (*She picks up Catherine's glass and drains it*) Now, concentrate: we owe Caxton five hundred. Correct?

CATHERINE. It seems so.

JANE. Brigette has just *given* us five hundred. Correct?

CATHERINE. Yes.

JANE. Brigette's a so-called friend. It's better to owe her rather than Caxton, who *isn't*.

(CATHERINE *is silent*)

Correct?

CATHERINE. You numb my brain when you're in this military mood.

JANE (*patiently*) She's only just given us the money; she won't expect immediate action as he does.

CATHERINE. I suppose that's correct.

JANE. Of course it is. (*She crosses to the door*) We'll get him paid and off our backs.

CATHERINE. One moment while I finish my drink. (*She sees her glass is empty and reaches for Jane's glass*) Oh! I'll have yours.

JANE (*moving quickly to the table below the sofa and picking up her drink*) No, you won't. I need it.

CATHERINE. Oh! Do you think it's wise?

JANE. Yes. (*She swallows her drink*) Oh! I'm not so sure. Never mind, too late. (*She replaces the glass on the table and crosses to the door*)

CATHERINE (*rising and moving up R of the sofa*) Jane, wait! Remember; when you tried to pay him back before, you got more.

JANE. The day you remember something cheerful I'll propose to Caxton.

(JANE *opens the door and suddenly comes face to face with* CAXTON)

Good evening. (*She turns and crosses to* L *of Catherine*)

CAXTON (*crossing to* L *of Jane*) Sorry to pop in again.

JANE (*moving below the desk*) It's a most convenient pop.

(CATHERINE *crosses and closes the door*)

CAXTON (*moving above the sofa and putting his brief-case on it*) I won't be a jiff. But as I drove home I started thinking about all this Portuguese business, and I decided to come back as there's so much that worries me.

CATHERINE (*moving* LC) Worries you!

CAXTON (*firmly*) I want more details.

JANE (*moving above the right end of the sofa; the gin taking effect*) I don't think I heard that correctly.

CAXTON (*moving to* L *of Jane*) I said I want more details: dates, names and addresses, et cetera.

JANE. Et cetera—why?

CAXTON. It's my right: I have a lot of cash involved.

JANE (*moving to the desk chair; grandly*) Mr Caxton. I gather from your tone that you don't trust us.

CAXTON (*moving up* L *of the desk*) Oh, come now, dear—Mrs Hayling.

CATHERINE. We've sensed it before and it's distressed us exceedingly.

CAXTON (*crossing to* R *of Catherine*) I'm only saying that . . .

JANE (*sitting at the desk; interrupting*) So much so that we have decided to tear up your cheque. (*She shuffles through the mass of papers on the desk*) If I can find it; and write you another for the odd hundred —if I can find the cheque-book.

CAXTON (*agitatedly moving between Jane and Catherine and finishing above the sofa; upset*) Here, here, what's all this? I trust you like my own dear ones. It's just that as I'd never actually seen the jewels, or the Portuguese lady; or the receipts . . .

JANE (*still searching*) You'd never think we were the tidy people we are. I had it in my hand only a moment ago. Gin's delicious, but it does slow one up. (*She picks up Brigette's cheque*) Oh, here's one for five hundred.

(CAXTON *moves up* L *of the desk*)

I'll endorse that over to you, and we can stop playing hunt the slipper. (*She searches for a pen*)

(CAXTON *picks up the cheque*)

CAXTON (*studying the cheque*) "Five hundred pounds, Brigette Blair." That's Mrs Brigette Blair.

CATHERINE (*aghast*) Jane, what have you done?

CAXTON (*demandingly*) What has she given you this for?

JANE (*grandly*) That's neither hither nor thither.

CAXTON (*again moving between Jane and Catherine, hardly knowing which one to address; accusingly*) It's a deposit on the emeralds. That's why you're so anxious to get rid of me.

CATHERINE. If that's what you choose to think . . .

CAXTON. You can't do this to me: I'll have the law on you. In any case you'd be crazy to sell to Mrs Blair. (*He moves up L of the desk*) She's known in the trade to be as mean as a fiddler's bitch.

JANE (*rising and crossing above Caxton to R of Catherine*) Mr Caxton, you'll get nowhere by insulting our friends.

CATHERINE. We never said we were selling to Mrs Blair.

CAXTON (*moving to R of Jane*) Then why is this cheque made out to Mrs Hayling?

(JANE and CATHERINE *are both stumped for a moment, then* JANE *speaks with the calm of alcoholic invention*)

JANE. I have already told you, Mr Caxton, that we are not the *only* Mrs Haylings.

CAXTON. You mean Number Three's over here?

JANE. I was amazed when Mrs Blair handed us this cheque saying, "As soon as she arrives, give this to—Conchita."

CAXTON (*turning away*) I didn't know she was coming over.

CATHERINE. Neither did I.

JANE. She's evidently grown tired of the perpetual smell of fish in Portugal. (*She nudges Catherine*)

CATHERINE (*catching on; uncertainly*) And the smell of paint. They're having their beautiful Byzantine house done up. Hand carved lace, like stone.

JANE. Then she was shocked by the underwear always hanging up in the streets.

CATHERINE. So she boarded a plane this morning.

JANE. And started these negotiations with Brigette of which we knew nothing.

CAXTON (*falsely*) You must forgive me, dear—Mrs Haylings, for having my doubts. I'm as happy as pie now that I can negotiate straight with Mrs . . . What did you say her present name was?

JANE. "Conchita."

CAXTON. I can hardly be that familiar. Her married name?

JANE (*panicking*) Er . . . You want to know her married name? Now—now, what is it? I always forget these fiddly foreign names. (*Leaving Catherine holding the baby*) Catherine, dear—(*she moves down L of the table L*) tell him her married name.

CATHERINE (*moving to R of the table L*) Surely you remember. (*She gazes around the room for inspiration. To Caxton*) I don't know how she's ever going to learn a long role on the television. (*She catches sight of the box of plums*) Elvas! Remember now? Senhora Conchita Elvas.

JANE. Of course. (*She slams down the lid of the box*) Such a lovely fruity name.

CAXTON (*moving down* R *of the sofa*) When can I meet Mrs Elvas?
JANE (*moving* LC) You can't.
CAXTON (*crossing to* R *of Jane and waving the cheque*) Why not?
JANE (*snatching the cheque and retreating down* L) She—has to return to Portugal. (*She mimes and treads across to* R *of the sofa*) It's the time of the treading of the grapes.
CAXTON (*nastily*) Mightn't it be for another reason altogether?
CATHERINE (*moving up* R *of Caxton*) What do you mean?
CAXTON (*crossing slowly to the stool*) I'm beginning to have a nasty little suspicion that you've cooked up this Mrs Elvas to fob me off because you think Brigette Blair'll pay more.
JANE (*angry with alarm*) How dare you make such an accusation.
CATHERINE. It's monstrous.
JANE (*crossing to the door and opening it*) Be so kind as to leave our house immediately. (*She stands above the doorway*)

(CATHERINE *crosses and stands below the doorway*)

CATHERINE. Yes.
CAXTON. Now, now, dears, don't take it so hard.
JANE. We do, Mr Caxton, we take it flint hard.
CAXTON (*craftily*) Perhaps I was wrong to have doubted Mrs Elvas.
CATHERINE. There's no "perhaps" about it.
CAXTON (*clearly*) After all, I've only got to ask Mrs Blair about her.
JANE (*moving to* L *of the sofa; so alarmed that she is furious*) No. No! That we will not have.
CATHERINE (*moving to* L *of Jane*) No, we won't.
CAXTON (*nastily*) But if she exists and is here . . .
JANE (*moving to* L *of Caxton; loudly*) If we say she's here, she *is* here. And we won't have you snooping round daring to doubt our word. (*She snaps her fingers in Caxton's face, then turns and moves above the sofa towards the door*)
CAXTON (*slightly abashed by her fury*) It's just that I wanted to meet your Mrs Elvas.
JANE (*turning to face Caxton; loud in her anger*) Very well! You shall meet her.
CATHERINE (*sitting on the sofa at the left end*) Jane!
JANE. I'll arrange for her to be here on Wednesday at three. Will that suit?
CAXTON. Oh, yes, ta. Much obliged.
JANE (*moving up* L *of Caxton and wagging a finger at him*) Then make a note; tea at three, with Number Three.

JANE *winks at Catherine as——*

the CURTAIN *falls*

ACT III

Scene—*The same. The following Wednesday afternoon.*

When the Curtain *rises,* Catherine *is seated on the sofa, expectantly facing the door. The door is suddenly flung open.* Rose *enters and stands to one side.*

Rose (*announcing importantly*) Senhora Elvas.
Catherine. Now you've left out the Christian name.
Rose. Would you believe it?
Catherine (*resignedly*) Go on, try again.
Rose. Well, don't watch me this time: it puts me off.

(Rose *exits, closing the door, then immediately re-enters*)

Ready?
Catherine. Yes, of course. Hurry!

(Rose *exits, closing the door, then opens it with a flourish and re-enters*)

Rose (*laboriously announcing*) Senhora—Conkita . . .
Catherine. Conchita! Cheetah—like the animal.
Rose. Wait a sec. I'll start again.

(Rose *exits, then immediately re-enters*)

Rose. Senhora—Conchita . . . Bless me if I haven't forgotten the other part, now.
Catherine (*rising and shouting*) Like the plums. Like the plums.
Rose. I've told you: I've never heard of them. Shout like that, and I'll announce Senhora Plum. Then you'll be in the soup.
Catherine. Elvas. (*Slowly*) Sen-hora Con-chita El-vas.

(Rose *exits, then immediately re-enters*)

Rose. Sen-hora Con-chita El-vas. (*Triumphantly*) There!
Catherine. It'll have to do, I suppose. (*She looks at her watch, moves towards the window, glances out, then moves up R of the sofa*) I haven't felt so anxious since I waited at the church for Basil.
Rose (*moving below the sofa*) Now, don't worry, dear. She'll carry it off to a T. She's a very good actress is Mrs Jane: I once saw her as Nell Gwynn.
Catherine (*moving to R of Rose*) We don't want anything like Nell Gwynn. The little Jane knows about Portugal comes from a very out-of-date guide-book.
Rose. That'll be enough to give her ideas.
Catherine. That's what I'm afraid of! It took all my tact—(*with tongue against teeth*) to sthop her lithping everything. Still, what we've thought of will silence Caxton once and for all, if she can carry it off.

Rose. I'll help all I can: "build up her entrance", as she calls it.

Catherine. No, no, you mustn't encourage her. (*She crosses down* L) Oh, dear! I have a horrible foreboding that something will go wrong. (*She moves to* L *of Rose*) In case it does, we must have an emergency action.

Rose. Oh, yes, let's.

Catherine. If disaster looms, I'll—tap on the floor. (*She demonstrates with her foot*) Like this. If you're in the dining-room you should hear it.

Rose. I'll stand on the table.

Catherine. You're a tower of strength.

Rose. But what do I do?

Catherine. You hasten up and—cause a diversion.

Rose. Say the house is on fire?

Catherine. No, no, nothing as drastic as that. Just come in and . . .

(*The sound of a door slamming is heard*)

What's that?

Rose. Front door. Perhaps it's her already. (*She goes to the door and looks off*)

(Catherine *follows to* R *of Rose*)

No, it's Master Philip and Mrs Dawson.

Catherine (*horrified*) What! But they're at the cinema.

Rose. Then it's their ghosts.

Catherine. They mustn't see Jane as Conchita. It would ruin everything. Quickly. Go and keep guard while I get rid of them again. If Mrs Jane arrives, tell her to go on driving round in the taxi.

(Susan *and* Philip *enter.* Rose *moves down* L)

Philip (*crossing to* L *of Catherine*) Hullo, Mother.

Catherine. Why aren't you at the cinema? (*She gestures to Rose*)

(Rose *exits*)

Susan (*moving to* L *of Philip*) We found it had been on a quarter of an hour so we decided not to bother.

Catherine. Of course you must bother. It's a superb film. May alter the whole course of your lives. Off you go.

Philip (*crossing below the desk*) If we wait a few weeks it'll come to the local, and we'll see it at half price.

Catherine (*moving below the sofa; almost shouting*) But I've given you the whole price. Go and see it now.

Philip. What on earth's the matter with you, Mother?

Catherine. Your vacillation. (*She moves towards the window, then turns suddenly above the sofa*) The roses will be out in Kew Gardens: go and look at them.

PHILIP. We don't want to look at anything. My final exam's in a month: Mrs Dawson's going to help me get my notes in order. (*He moves to the bureau*)

(SUSAN *closes the door, then crosses to* L *of Philip*)

CATHERINE. Not in here.

PHILIP. I think one of my first-year notebooks is in this thing.

CATHERINE (*moving below the sofa*) Well, hurry! I have an appointment in ten minutes.

(CATHERINE *moves distractedly about down* C, *while* PHILIP *searches in the bureau cupboard and extracts a notebook*)

PHILIP (*apprehensively*) You couldn't spare me five of them? I rather want to talk to you about something.

CATHERINE. If it's something that will take my mind off—where it is, I'd be glad.

PHILIP. It'll do that all right. But it may be rather a shock.

CATHERINE (*sitting on the sofa*) Nothing could shock me any more.

PHILIP (*to Susan*) Then I think now's the time. Do you mind?

SUSAN. I shall be most relieved. (*She moves to* L *of the stool*)

PHILIP (*crossing to* R *of Catherine*) Mother, there is now a third Mrs Hayling.

CATHERINE (*sitting up in a panic*) You know? Horror! Who else does?

SUSAN. No-one. We've kept it a complete secret.

CATHERINE. Thank Heavens. If anyone else discovers, we're ruined.

SUSAN. But you're not.

CATHERINE (*rising and moving down* LC) She's been nothing but trouble from the very beginning.

PHILIP. Mother, I won't have you saying that.

CATHERINE. We must take drastic action. For the present we'll give out that she's disappeared.

SUSAN. Disappeared!

CATHERINE. Then later on, we'll kill her off.

PHILIP. Mother!

SUSAN (*moving to* R *of Philip*) It was a terrible shock: we should have broken it gradually.

CATHERINE (*moving to* L *of Philip*) The trouble is that Jane loves her and won't want her done away with.

PHILIP. You've been drinking.

CATHERINE. Only a thimbleful of *crème de menthe* to help me face this terrible afternoon. (*She crosses and looks in the mirror on the wall down* L).

PHILIP. You never must again. (*He takes Susan by the hand and crosses to* LC *with her*) Now, pull yourself together, and realize that Susan and I are married.

CATHERINE. Married! Oh, I see. (*She moves to* L *of them*) But you said you had no intention of even asking her.

PHILIP. Because I'd *already* asked her, darling. We've been married since before she came to live here.

SUSAN (*crossing to R of Catherine*) We loved each other so much, and having no money and nowhere to live it seemed the only solution.

CATHERINE (*panic-stricken*) But if you're married you won't get your father's legacy!

PHILIP. It's all right; we shall. I raised some cash, and engaged a very crafty lawyer who says the marriage clause can be got round.

CATHERINE. Is he sure?

PHILIP. He seemed pretty sure.

CATHERINE (*suddenly*) How did you raise this money?

PHILIP (*awkwardly*) The writing-table.

CATHERINE (*pointing to the desk*) That writing-table?

PHILIP (*quickly*) Don't worry, we shan't lose it. We can pay him off when we get the legacy. He only advanced it in case we might want to sell one day.

CATHERINE. That phrase rings a horrible bell. Not Mr Caxton?

PHILIP. Yes.

CATHERINE. The double-faced monster.

(ROSE *enters, crosses and stands between Catherine and Susan. She carries a sealed brown-paper wrapped parcel.* PHILIP *and* SUSAN *move a little* C)

ROSE. Mrs Catherine, "Part One" is here.

CATHERINE. What?

ROSE (*very distinctly*) "Part One" is here.

PHILIP. Who?

CATHERINE (*quickly*) It's all right. I know.

ROSE (*handing the parcel to Catherine*) And this came by registered post.

CATHERINE. It's from the Polish watchmaker. It would arrive now. I shall go mad. Keep it, and guard it with your life. (*She hands the parcel to Rose*) And send up "Part One" after you've counted twenty—slowly. (*She marks Rose's hand, and starts counting*) One, two . . .

ROSE (*counting*) Three, four, five . . .

(ROSE, *counting slowly aloud and walking in time, exits, leaving the door open*)

PHILIP. What is going on, Mother?

CATHERINE. Something only I can cope with. Run along, both of you and—celebrate.

SUSAN. You're not completely furious?

CATHERINE. If things are ever calmer, I think I shall be delighted. (*She kisses Susan*) But go now, and don't come in here again till I call you.

PHILIP (*crossing below Susan to R of Catherine*) But who is this "Part One"?

CATHERINE. Suppose it was Fiona?
PHILIP. What!

(PHILIP *grabs* SUSAN *by the hand and they rush out*)

CATHERINE (*moving to the door and shouting after them*) Whatever you do, don't say a word to anyone about anything. (*She closes the door, stands in bewilderment for a moment, then hurries to the bureau, takes a bottle of crème de menthe and a glass from the cupboard, and pours herself a drink. She drinks, then replaces the bottle and glass in the cupboard*)

(ROSE *enters and stands to one side*)

ROSE (*announcing*) Mr Caxton.

(CAXTON *enters and crosses below the sofa.*
ROSE *exits, closing the door*)

CAXTON. Well, here's the repentant bad penny. Hope I'm not the early worm, as well?
CATHERINE. Well, Senhora Elvas hasn't arrived yet. Jane's gone to fetch her from *Claridges*. (*She crosses to* R *of Caxton*) This is her first visit to London, and she has no bump of location.
CAXTON. If you'd let me know, I could have gone there.
CATHERINE. We thought it safer—(*she corrects herself*) more convenient, here. (*She looks at the clock on the bureau, then moves towards the window and glances out*) It's well after three. What can have happened to her—them?
CAXTON (*crossing to* L *of the desk*) Shall we ring *Claridges*?
CATHERINE (*moving quickly above the sofa; frantically*) No, no! (*She explains*) Portuguese are notoriously unpunctual.
CAXTON (*sitting on the sofa at the right end and rubbing his hands*) Knowing both of you, I'm agog to see what she's like.
CATHERINE. Well, please don't stare: their code of behaviour is much stricter than ours.
CAXTON (*hurt*) I know; I've travelled.
CATHERINE. Conchita's quite different in character, but Basil rather kept to one type.
CAXTON. Oh?
CATHERINE. Conchita, Jane and I have often been mistaken for each other.
CAXTON. I wouldn't have thought you and the other Mrs Hayling were much alike. Not in broad daylight, anyhow.
CATHERINE. Perhaps not so much in broad daylight. (*She looks anxiously at the sun pouring through the windows*) That reminds me! Conchita's very susceptible to glare. I think I'll lower the blinds a little. (*She moves towards the window*)

(ROSE *enters excitedly*)

ROSE. Your famous guest is here!
CATHERINE (*moving above the sofa; very nervous*) Oh! Well, bring her straight up, please.

Rose. She's a lovely lady. Shouldn't be surprised if she had royal blood in her veins.

Catherine. Really. Show her up.

Rose. Oh, yes. I can just see her at the bullfight with a carnation tucked behind her ear.

Catherine (*alarmed, and speaking very firmly*) You'll see the inside of an old ladies' home if you don't show her up immediately.

Rose. Wait a sec. I think I hear her coming.

(Rose *exits*)

Catherine. Rose's ideas of abroad are coloured by frequent visits to the cinema.

(Rose, *in order that everything shall be as rehearsed, quickly closes the door so that she can straightaway fling it open and announce stentoriously.*
    Rose *enters and stands above the open doorway*)

Rose (*announcing*) Senhora Conchita Elvas.

(*There is a moment's pause.*
    Jane *enters. She is almost unrecognizable and is dressed magnificently as her idea of a Portuguese lady of title. She speaks with a strong accent, and carries a bunch of red roses tied with red ribbon.* Catherine *moves down* R *of* Jane. Caxton *rises and moves down* R *of the sofa*)

Jane. Greetings from your oldest ally!

Catherine. Conchita, my dear.

Jane. Catterina, my dearer.

(*They kiss elaborately from one cheek to the other*)

(*She presents the roses to Catherine*) For you. (*She turns to Rose*) Little Rosa. How you've grown.

Catherine (*putting the roses on the chair up* C) May I present Senhor Julius Caxton.

Jane (*with a half curtsy*) Senhor, I am ravished. (*She moves below the sofa and holds out her hand to Caxton*)

(Rose *moves* LC)

Caxton (*embarrassed*) The pleasure's mine, I'm sure.

Jane. You do not kiss the hand in Britain?

Caxton. Oh, of course, pardon. (*He kisses Jane's hand*)

Jane (*holding out her other hand*) Now, you may do the other one.

Caxton. Ta. (*He kisses Jane's other hand*)

(Rose *stares at* Jane)

Jane (*moving to* R *of* Rose) Grathios.

(Rose *continues to stare*)

Grathios. That means you're excused.

Rose. It's all right, I've nothing to do.

Jane. Then find something to do, quick

(Rose *exits angrily, closing the door*)

(*She turns to Caxton with a dazzling smile*) In Portugal we say, "Idle woman never become mistress." Very true, yes?

CAXTON. Very nicely put.

JANE (*moving below the sofa and flashing her eyes at Caxton*) I am entranced you like it.

CATHERINE (*moving R of the table L*) But, Conchita dear, where is Jane?

JANE. I am asking where is Jane. I wait for her as appointed, but she disappointed.

CAXTON. Didn't she come and collect you?

JANE. You mean I am a parcel?

CAXTON. No, no.

JANE (*again flashing her eyes at him*) Very nice parcel, yes?

CAXTON. And a very smart one.

JANE (*smoothing her dress*) Little woman round Estoril corner.

CATHERINE. I wonder if Jane went to the wrong hotel: she's very scatter-brained.

JANE (*angrily*) Not at all. She is very charming. Beautiful and intelligent. (*To Caxton*) Do you not agree?

CAXTON. Well . . .

JANE. I knew you would. You come and sit by me. (*She sits on the sofa*)

(CAXTON *sits R of Jane on the sofa*)

We shall be great friends. Come one day and see me at *Ritz Hotel*. (*She crosses her knees and pulls her skirt a little higher*)

CATHERINE. *Claridges Hotel*, dearest.

JANE. Your pardon?

CATHERINE (*pointedly*) I'd just been telling Mr Caxton about your staying at *Claridges*.

JANE. How stupid!

CATHERINE. Conchita, dearest.

JANE (*with her sweetest smile*) Stupid not to remember only first night at *Claridges*, then removing to *Ritz*.

CATHERINE. Oh, of course. (*She moves the chair from L to R of the table L, and sits*) That explains what has happened to Jane, too.

JANE (*to Caxton; with a dazzling smile*) Usually I bed down with their Excellencies at Embassy.

CAXTON. But Mrs Hayling was telling me this is your first visit to London.

JANE. Mrs Hayling talk too much.

CATHERINE. Conchita, my love.

JANE. My other visits were incognito. I come often: I adore your capital.

CAXTON. How does it compare with your own capital?

JANE (*at a complete loss*) My own capital? I must think about my own capital.

CATHERINE (*stepping into the breach*) I expect it's difficult to compare two such cities?

JANE. It is impossible.

CAXTON (*rising*) Well, now we've done the social, let's get down to brass tacks.

JANE (*to Catherine*) What is it he say? Brass tacks?

CATHERINE. He's referring to the emeralds, dear.

JANE (*pretending anger*) You call my emeralds brass tacks. (*She rises and crosses to the door*) I leave!

(CATHERINE *rises*)

CAXTON. No, no—(*he rises and crosses to L*) it was only a manner of speaking.

JANE (*crossing above the sofa to R of it*) I do not like your manner of speaking. Brass tacks!

(CAXTON *crosses below the sofa*)

Emeralds are mossy green pools. Larger than the Shah of Persia's. (*She moves down R of the sofa, then crosses below Caxton to R of Catherine*)

CATHERINE. Careful, dear. Don't exaggerate too much. (*She replaces the chair L, then moves to R of the table L*)

CAXTON (*crossing to R of Jane; strongly*) Look, Madam Elvas. I've handed out a lot of money on these emeralds. I want first to see them. And then to buy them.

JANE. In Portugal we say, "Loud man needs tongue cut." (*She makes a snipping gesture near Caxton's mouth*)

CAXTON (*moving down R of the sofa*) I'm only trying to state my case.

JANE (*crossing to L of Caxton*) Then stop stating it. And listen while I state mine. (*She turns away to R of Catherine*)

CATHERINE. Careful, dear, don't be too—Portuguese.

JANE (*moving to L of Caxton*) Emeralds are eggs, veritable bantam's eggs. (*She crosses below Caxton to L of the stool*)

CAXTON (*moving to L of Jane; furiously*) I didn't come here to talk about bantams.

JANE (*pretending to be furious*) And I didn't come here to talk to a man with nothing up here—(*she touches her head*) and everything— (*she gestures in front of her stomach*) down here.

(CAXTON *moves below the sofa.* CATHERINE *crosses above the sofa to* L *of Jane and tries to calm her. The following is more or less ad lib.*)

I do not like this man, great big insulting man, *etc.*

CATHERINE. Let us all be friends. What about a smile?

JANE. I do not feel like smiling. I can't smile when I do not feel smile. Why should I? *etc.*

(CATHERINE *eventually manages to get a big smile from* JANE *and they embrace*)

CATHERINE. Now, let us all sit down, and talk it over quietly.

(Jane *sits on the sofa.* Caxton *sits* l *of Jane on the sofa*)

(*She sits on the stool*) Tell Mr Caxton what we've arranged, Conchita dear.

JANE. Yes. Well, Senhor Caxton, there is a lot about these emeralds which is unsatisfactory

CAXTON. There I agree.

JANE. Now, listen and listen carefully. (*Very distinctly*) We have decided to cancel all previous transactions. I am going to buy Jane and Catterina's shares, and I shall take the emeralds to Portugal.

CATHERINE. We accept your generous offer.

CAXTON. Now, wait a minute . . .

JANE. Business over, now you have my permission to smoke.

CAXTON. I don't want to smoke.

JANE. I do. (*She takes a cheroot from her handbag*) Will you have one? They come from Portugal.

CAXTON. No, thanks, I don't care for cigars; they're too strong for me.

JANE. Fancy! In Portugal we say, "Man without cigar is like bull without horns." I love cigars.

(CAXTON *takes his lighter from his pocket and lights Jane's cheroot*)

(*She coughs a lot*) I love them! We all smoke cigars in Portugal.

CAXTON. Let us get back to the emeralds.

JANE. Emeralds are finished. Now I tell you about Portugal.

CAXTON (*rising*) But I want to talk about the emeralds.

JANE (*rising*) Do you know Portugal?

CAXTON. Can't say I do.

JANE. That's a relief. (*She adds hastily*) A relief that you should first hear of it from great patriot. (*She resumes her seat and pulls Caxton down beside her. In her best guide-book manner*) Portugal has a population of seven and three-quarter million.

CATHERINE. How interesting.

CAXTON. I know what you're up to. You're trying to sell to Mrs Blair.

JANE (*blowing smoke in Caxton's face to stop him talking*) Rivers, stocked with fish, flow through fine scenery dotted with windmills.

CAXTON (*pointing at Catherine*) But they've accepted five hundred pounds deposit from me.

JANE (*blowing another puff of smoke into Caxton's face*) Of great interest are the forests of oddly shaped cork trees—many of which have been denuded of their barks.

CAXTON. In any case, I'll give you a better price than Mrs Blair.

JANE (*silencing Caxton with another puff of smoke*) . . . many of which have been denuded of their barks. Be sure to visit the ancient town of Vila Real . . .

CAXTON (*rising; furiously*) I am not thinking of visiting Portugal at all.

JANE (*rising; firmly*) Then *do* think of it. Vila Real is birthplace

of world-famous navigator—world-famous navigator—whose name
—escapes me for the moment.

CATHERINE. We know who you mean, dear.

CAXTON. Senhora Elvas. Please understand I'm determined to
buy the emeralds.

JANE (*stopping Caxton with a puff of smoke*) In Lisboa—Lisbon—
there is a church with two Peruvian mummies—(*she demonstrates by
taking up a strange posture*) embalmed in a strange posture.

CAXTON (*crossing down* R; *to Catherine*) She doesn't seem to understand the danger you're all in.

CATHERINE (*rising and going down* L, *to avoid Caxton; nervously*) No,
talk to her, it's beyond me.

(*Caxton starts to follow Catherine*)

JANE (*relaxing from her pose and grabbing the back of Caxton's jacket*)
You have yet to hear of the bloodless bullfights.

(JANE *pulls* CAXTON *back to* R *of her and tosses her cigar on to the
floor* L. *She snatches his silk breast pocket handkerchief and demonstrates
the movements of a toreador whilst* CAXTON, *trying to get at his handkerchief involuntarily acts as the bull.* CATHERINE *picks up the cigar and puts
it in the ashtray on the table* L, *and watches nervously.* CAXTON *recovers
his handkerchief and crosses to* L *of the desk*)

CAXTON (*suddenly turning nasty*) Very well! (*He picks up the telephone
receiver*) I don't like to do it, but you've asked for it.

JANE (*moving below the sofa; to Catherine*) What is it we ask for?

CAXTON (*to Catherine*) Either you sell to me as you and the other
one promised, or I send for the police.

CATHERINE (*crossing to* L *of Caxton*) The police! No, Mr Caxton.

JANE. This is jest I do not care for.

CAXTON. This is no jest, lady. They entered into a contract with
me when they accepted my deposit. Either they honour it, or I
prosecute.

CATHERINE. This is calamitous. I think he means it. Do something.

JANE. I am. I go for afternoon siesta. (*She moves towards the door*)

CATHERINE (*following to* LC) No, no, Conchita! Stop him, some-
how.

(CAXTON, *still holding the telephone receiver which is on a long lead,
moves below the sofa*)

CAXTON. Look, I'm not fooling. It's either a sale, or the police.
Which?

JANE (*crossing and snatching the receiver from Caxton*) But to really
understand Portugal you must see her dance.

(JANE *gives an exhibition of Portuguese dancing and winds* CAXTON
*and herself in the telephone lead, and with a wild turn releases them both,
throwing the receiver to the floor.* CAXTON *sinks on to the stool, and* JANE
goes into a Spanish dance around him with arms waving and heels clicking.

Each time CAXTON *tries to rise to pick up the phone she steps smartly on his foot. When he tries to speak she bursts into fados-like singing. She finishes with an exaggerated pose, and sinks exhausted on to the sofa)*

CAXTON (*rising and picking up the receiver*) It's no good, lady. (*He moves to the desk and dials a number*) I'm getting on to Scotland Yard.

(CATHERINE *sits* L *of Jane on the sofa*)

JANE. Scotland Yard?
CAXTON. And that'll mean jail for all three.
JANE. Is he coming with us?
CAXTON (*into the telephone*) Hullo? Wait a moment, please. (*To Jane and Catherine*) This is your last chance. (*Still holding the receiver he moves below the sofa*)

(ROSE *enters excitedly*)

ROSE. There's been a disaster!
CATHERINE. What?
ROSE (*tapping her foot on the floor*) There's been a disaster.
CATHERINE (*rising and crossing down* L) Splendid! What is it?
ROSE. Come upstairs and look at me urgently.
CATHERINE. Come and look at you?
ROSE. I've got a rash all over my chest.
JANE (*rising*) A rash! Santa Eulialia. It's an epidemic. It kill thousands. I come. I come. (*She moves towards the door*)
CAXTON. I'm not letting you out of my sight.
JANE. Have you been vaccinated?
CAXTON. Vaccinated? No.
JANE. Santa Eulialia! Keep away, unclean, unclean! (*She screens her mouth and nose with the hem of her skirt*)

(JANE *and* CATHERINE *rush out.* ROSE *follows them off.* CAXTON *moves to the desk*)

CAXTON (*into the telephone; calmly*) Hullo, Momma? . . . This is Julius. My bluff has worked. They think I am on to the police. I'll bet you anything you like that they'll be back with the emeralds in ten minutes . . . (*Beaming*) Thank you, Momma. If they are as good as I think they are, I'll take you on a day trip to Bexhill. (*He replaces the receiver*)

(PHILIP *and* SUSAN *enter, leaving the door open*)

PHILIP (*moving* LC) What was all that noise, Mother? (*He sees Caxton*) Oh, it's you.

(SUSAN *moves to* L *of Philip*)

CAXTON (*crossing to* R *of Philip*) Ah, the very persons I wanted to see. What about my writing-table? Am I getting it?
SUSAN (*crossing and standing below the desk*) We told you we had to have time.

CAXTON. Not unending. There must be a limit. (*He crosses and closes the door*)

PHILIP (*crossing to* L *of Susan*) We're waiting the result of—a transaction. We'll give you a definite answer in about a fortnight.

CAXTON (*moving below the sofa*) No "about". (*Bitterly*) I'm beginning to know your family. A fortnight dead. I do this for a living not to amuse myself.

PHILIP (*crossing below Susan to the bureau*) All right, we'll let you know in a fortnight.

CAXTON. And no hanky-panky. (*He stands above the table* L) Remember you're under an obligation to sell.

(FIONA *enters and deliberately closes the door behind her*)

FIONA. Ah!

PHILIP. Fiona! I thought you were still in Portugal.

FIONA. Forgive the unannounced entra. But I didn't want the Houdina act again. (*She crosses to* L *of Susan*) I received an airmail that disturbed me even more than the Portuguese cooking. (*To Susan*) Is it true that you've beaten me to the altar with Phil?

SUSAN (*moving to* L *of Philip*) Well, to the registry office, yes. Some time ago.

PHILIP. I did try and put you off, Fiona. I couldn't actually tell you I was married because of father's will. I'm awfully sorry. (*He turns away down* R)

FIONA. Well, I'm not going to be so hippo as to say I don't mind. I do. I'm absolutely flabbers. But if you've got him, you've got him, I suppose.

SUSAN (*smiling*) I'm so sorry.

FIONA. For a year or two, anyhow. There's nil I can do but wait. (*Suddenly remembering*) Except claim my two hundred back from the girls.

PHILIP (*crossing to* R *of Fiona*) Two hundred?

FIONA. Pounds, my ex-love.

CAXTON (*crossing hurriedly to* L *of Fiona*) Two hundred pounds? What did you give them that for?

FIONA (*cuttingly*) If we've met it's slipped conveniently out of my memory. (*She crosses below Caxton and stands above the table* L)

CAXTON. Never mind the social. Have you been trying to buy their emeralds, too?

PHILIP. What emeralds?

CAXTON (*excitedly*) Now, now, come off it. You know very well what emeralds. The ones I've given your mothers five hundred on.

PHILIP. They haven't got any emeralds.

CAXTON (*slowly*) They haven't, eh?

SUSAN (*moving to* R *of Philip*) Your mother mentioned some to me, darling.

PHILIP. She did. (*To Caxton. Anxiously*) And you've advanced five hundred on them?

CAXTON. Yes, I have. Now, come on, have they got any, or have they made the whole thing up?

PHILIP (*crossing to the door*) I'd better find out, for all our sakes. (*To Susan*) Come and help me, darling.

(SUSAN *crosses to Philip*)

CAXTON. Better question Mrs Elvas, too.

SUSAN. Who?

CAXTON. Mrs Elvas.

(PHILIP *and* SUSAN *look puzzled*)

Elvas!

PHILIP (*shaking his head*) Suppose he means Rose.

(PHILIP *and* SUSAN *exit, closing the door.* FIONA *sits in the armchair down* L, *takes a cigarette from the box on the table and puts it in a long holder from her handbag*)

CAXTON (*moving to* R *of the table* L) So, milked you of two hundred, have they?

FIONA (*airily*) I don't understand dairy talk.

CAXTON. Oh, come off it. If you want to see your two hundred again, your only chance is to come in with me.

FIONA. I don't know where, but I can assure you I wouldn't for two thou.

CAXTON (*moving above the sofa*) I'd an idea from the beginning they'd invented the whole story.

FIONA. Then rather dim of you to follow through, wasn't it?

CAXTON. Ah, but by then I had seen all this furniture. I knew they wouldn't sell it just like that. (*He rubs his hands*) But now I've got them so they'll be forced to.

FIONA. If you ask me the whole biz sounds very dishon.

(ROSE *pops her head round the door*)

ROSE. You can stop worrying. It was a false alarm. It turned out to be bread-crumbs that had got down inside. (*She opens the door properly and announces*) Mrs Blair.

(CAXTON *moves down* R *of the sofa.*
BRIGETTE *enters. She is well wrapped in shawls, has a bad cold and speaks through her nose.*
ROSE *exits, closing the door*)

FIONA (*rising and moving to Brigette*) Thank Heav!

BRIGETTE. Don't come near me! I'm infectious. An appalling cold. (*She moves* LC)

FIONA (*crossing to the desk*) My dear! (*She lights her cigarette with the table-lighter, then moves above the sofa*)

BRIGETTE. I've only left my bed because I must see the girls on urgent business.

CAXTON (*crossing to* R *of Brigette*) Infectious or not, I'm pleased as pie to see you.

(BRIGETTE *takes her bottle and a tissue from her handbag and dabs her face*)

BRIGETTE. In my most extravagant reveries I never expected such a greeting from you.

CAXTON. Now look, dear. We must let bygones be bygones, and come to some agreement about this.

BRIGETTE. Influenza must be clogging my brain. What are you talking about?

CAXTON (*craftily*) The emeralds.

BRIGETTE. Then an agreement's utterly out of the question. (*She replaces the bottle in her bag*)

CAXTON (*immensely relieved*) Thank God there's something to have an agreement about.

BRIGETTE (*crossing to the desk*) I must have a temperature. (*She throws the tissue into the waste-paper basket*)

FIONA. He's abnor, I think.

CAXTON (*moving below the left end of the sofa*) What's your ceiling price?

BRIGETTE (*moving below the right end of the sofa*) I couldn't possibly know without seeing them.

(FIONA *stands above the sofa between the others, looking from one to the other in turn*)

CAXTON (*aghast*) You mean, you haven't seen them?

BRIGETTE. I knew you'd see them.

CAXTON. I haven't seen them.

BRIGETTE. You haven't seen them!

FIONA (*to Caxton*) Your service.

BRIGETTE (*anxiously*) You do know there are some emeralds, though, don't you?

CAXTON. I've always had my doubts. (*Puzzled*) Yet that Mrs Elvas was keen enough to get them.

BRIGETTE. Who?

CAXTON. Your Portuguese friend, Mrs Elvas.

BRIGETTE (*turning away down* R) I'm not well enough to joke.

CAXTON (*getting excited*) Ah, you're in it, too, eh? They *do* exist, you've seen them, and are just helping to get rid of me.

BRIGETTE (*moving below the sofa*) Don't you talk that way to me.

CAXTON (*retreating above the table* L) Be careful; I can soon fix you.

(PHILIP *and* SUSAN *enter, leaving the door open.* PHILIP *stands down* L *of the sofa with* SUSAN L *of him*)

Now we shall know the truth.

BRIGETTE. Philip, I must see the girls urgently. Where are they?

SUSAN. We don't know.

PHILIP (*worried*) We've searched the house, and there's no sign of either of them.

SUSAN. They've completely vanished.

BRIGETTE. Vanished?

FIONA (*moving below the desk*) What a lark: they've welched.

CAXTON (*almost demented with worry*) They're probably half way to America by now.

BRIGETTE. Oh, be quiet. (*To Philip*) What's the truth about the emeralds?

PHILIP (*looking at Susan*) I'm not sure.

(*The following scene must build to a crescendo of babble*)

CAXTON (*moving above the sofa*) Well, at least they couldn't take any of the furniture with them.

PHILIP (*crossing to the window*) I'd better go out and see if there's any sign of them.

FIONA (*moving quickly to the window*) I hope they haven't driven away in my bubble.

(SUSAN *crosses to* L *of Philip.* BRIGETTE *moves to* R *of the table* L)

CAXTON. I was the first to pay out, so I've got first claim on everything I want.

SUSAN (*crossing to* L *of Caxton*) Please don't get so excited. There's probably a perfectly natural explanation.

BRIGETTE (*crossing to the telephone and lifting the receiver*) I wonder if there's any possible hope they haven't cashed my cheque. (*She dials a number*)

FIONA (*moving to* L *of Brigette*) Oughtn't we to ring up Scotters?

CAXTON (*rubbing his hands and indicating various pieces of furniture*) Besides the writing-table I'll have that, and that, and all these.

PHILIP (*turning at the window; angrily*) Shut up!

SUSAN. Please let's think what to do *quietly*.

CAXTON (*to Susan*) You can come very well out of this. I'll tell you what I'll do . . .

(PHILIP *moves between Caxton and Susan.*

ROSE *enters and stands above the open doorway. She holds the brown-paper parcel*)

ROSE (*at the top of her voice*) If you'll keep quiet——

(*They are silent*)

—(*in a firm low voice*) I have a message.

(PHILIP *crosses to* R *of Rose.* BRIGETTE *replaces the receiver and moves below the desk*)

They realize they have to pay the penalty. (*She gives the parcel to Philip*) These will speak for themselves. And you're to ring up a taxi as they don't want to be seen in a Black Maria.

(ROSE *exits, closing the door*)

CAXTON. What does all that mean in plain English?

PHILIP. I'm not sure.

BRIGETTE (*moving below the sofa*) What's in the parcel, Philip?

PHILIP. I don't know.

SUSAN. Isn't it the one your mother had just now from the Polish watchmaker?

CAXTON. Polish watchmaker? (*Very excited*) That's them, then—that's them.

BRIGETTE. Them? The emeralds?

FIONA. Good Heav!

CAXTON. Quick! Let me see them, let me see them.

PHILIP. No. They're nothing to do with you.

CAXTON. What do you mean—nothing to do with me? I've paid five hundred pounds deposit on them.

BRIGETTE. So have I. Come on, Philip, we must clear this up immediately.

PHILIP (*turning the packet in his hands*) I must say I'd like to see what you've paid out on.

FIONA. I must say dit.

CAXTON. What are we waiting for, then? (*He snatches the parcel from Philip, crosses, sits at the desk and opens the parcel*)

(FIONA *moves down* R *of the desk.* BRIGETTE *moves to* L *of Caxton.* SUSAN *moves to* L *of Brigette*)

PHILIP (*crossing to* L *of Susan*) I knew they were up to something, but this exceeds even their limit.

BRIGETTE. If they're good—(*with meaning*) and *I* get them, it means a holiday in the Argentine for you both.

(CAXTON *takes an emerald spray from the parcel. They all exclaim at its brilliance*)

FIONA. But, my dears, it's absolutely daz.

CAXTON (*inspecting it*) Gold setting. Not worth the melting value.

BRIGETTE. The stones look an exquisite colour.

CAXTON. Half a jiff! (*He takes a jeweller's eyeglass from his pocket and screws it into his eye*) We'll soon tell. (*He studies the emeralds*)

SUSAN (*to Philip*) You see, they did exist.

PHILIP (*moving to the window*) I don't understand.

CAXTON. Hullo, hullo. What's this? Look at the backs. They've been painted.

FIONA. Painted?

(PHILIP *returns to* L *of Susan*)

PHILIP ⎫   ⎧ Painted?
SUSAN ⎬ (*together*) ⎨ What for?
BRIGETTE ⎭   ⎩ That's what I feared.

CAXTON. Have you got anything we could dissolve the varnish with?

BRIGETTE. I have! My alcohol. (*She takes the bottle from her handbag and puts it on the desk*)

CAXTON. Ideal. (*He takes a pair of tweezers from his pocket*) I'll dismount one, then we'll soon see. (*He indicates the bottle*) Some in that ashtray, please.

(BRIGETTE *pours some alcohol into the ashtray.* FIONA *produces some cotton-wool from her handbag.* CAXTON *extracts one of the emeralds and washes it in the spirit*)

SUSAN. Is it melting it?

CAXTON. It's thick—absolutely plastered on.

FIONA. I'm so excited I've got the palps.

CAXTON. Nearly all off, now. Let's see. Put that light on.

(PHILIP *moves to the standard lamp and switches it on*)

(*He studies the jewel*) Yes . . .

PHILIP. Yes, what?

BRIGETTE. Paint only put on to enrich the colour?

CAXTON. Yes. It's a paler stone, now. (*With great satisfaction*) But still excellent.

BRIGETTE (*snatching the stone from Caxton*) Let me look. Oh—but remarkable. Delicious. One of the finest I've ever seen.

CAXTON (*snatching the stone from Brigette*) Yes, exceptional. (*He realizes he has given too much away*) At least—quite good.

BRIGETTE. Let me see the rest of it.

(FIONA *picks up the spray and holds it against herself.* BRIGETTE *reaches across and takes the spray from Fiona.*

JANE *and* CATHERINE *enter. They each wear a fur coat and carry a small grip.* CATHERINE *is* L *of Jane*)

JANE. But I'm sure they *provide* nightdresses in Holloway, Catherine.

BRIGETTE (*moving down* L *of the desk*) My dear girls. There you are.

SUSAN (*moving above the sofa*) Mrs Hayling. We've been worried stiff.

(CAXTON *rises*)

PHILIP (*crossing to* R *of Jane*) Where on earth have you been?

JANE. In the attic. To fetch our fur coats. We're going on a long visit.

CATHERINE (*crossing to the bureau*) And fear the place will be damp and cold.

(JANE *moves below the sofa and puts down her grip.* PHILIP *moves down* L *of the sofa*)

JANE (*to Susan*) I hope you don't mind: I've packed your hot-water bottle as well as my own.

CAXTON (*moving below the right end of the sofa; unctuously*) Before you go anywhere, my dears, we've got to have a little talk on business. Where's Mrs Elvas?

JANE. She became hysterical; we sent her away in an ambulance. (*She moves to the table L and tips the contents of the cigarette box into her grip*) These are to bribe the warders.

PHILIP. Mother, what is all this about emeralds?

CATHERINE. You'll hear all about it at the trial. But now we've got to finish packing. (*She takes the bottle of crème de menthe from the bureau cupboard and puts it into her grip. To Jane*) Shall we take writing-paper and envelopes?

JANE (*crossing to the desk*) I think we're only allowed one letter a week. (*She picks up the table-lighter and puts it into her grip*) But put in postcards. We could have great fun with them. "Wish you were here. 'X' marks my cell."

PHILIP. For Heaven's sake . . .

BRIGETTE. Now, listen . . .

CATHERINE (*crossing and kissing Brigette*) Brigette dear, on visiting days bring lots of fresh fruit. (*She kisses Susan and Philip, then crosses to the door*)

JANE (*moving below the sofa; to Brigette*) See if you can smuggle us in some cold cream, Brigette. Our fingers will be awful if it's mail-bags.

CATHERINE (*interrupting with a scream*) Our hair. Suppose they cut it all off?

JANE (*crossing with her grip to the door*) We're going to prison, darling, not a convent.

PHILIP (*shouting*) You're not going to prison, or a convent, or anywhere else.

SUSAN. The emeralds are real.

JANE (*putting her grip on the table L*) My heart's stopped.

CATHERINE (*crossing to L of Caxton*) You're joking.

CAXTON. They're talking copper-bottomed truth, dear Mrs Haylings.

CATHERINE. Not fakes?

CAXTON. No. In fact, the stones are not at all bad. So I'll tell you what I'll do.

JANE (*crossing below Catherine to L of Caxton*) I know! Be absolutely honest with us.

(ROSE *runs in to L of Catherine*)

ROSE (*as she enters*) Help! I've swallowed my plate.

JANE. Nonsense, no-one could swallow a plate.

ROSE. But I have!

CATHERINE. Don't be silly, Rose.

CAXTON. Listen, I'm prepared to give you another five hundred pounds down, and three thousand more if the confirmatory tests are satisfactory.

BRIGETTE (*crossing below Caxton to R of Jane*) Damn confirmatory tests. I'll give you another three thousand five hundred pounds this very minute, making it four thousand pounds.

PHILIP. It's not enough.

ROSE. I was eating a piece of toffee . . .

JANE. Oh, do go away, Rose.

CATHERINE. Don't let's do anything in a rush . . .

FIONA (*crossing below Caxton and Brigette to* R *of Jane; shouting above the noise*) As I can't have Phil, I'm determined to have something I like. I bid four thousand two hundred pounds.

JANE (*removing her fur coat and climbing on to the sofa*) This lady bids me four thousand two hundred pounds. Any advance on four thousand two hundred?

There is a chorus of voices bidding excitedly as - - -

the CURTAIN *slowly falls*

FURNITURE AND PROPERTY LIST

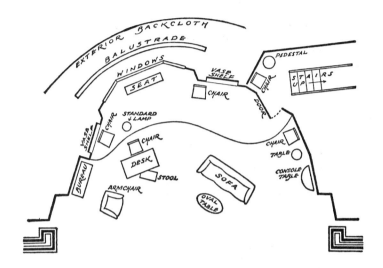

ACT I

On stage: Console table. *On it:* vase of flowers
On wall over console table: trick moulded mirror
Round table (L)
Upright chair (L)
On wall over upright chair L: movable picture (flower painting)
Sofa. *On it:* cushions
Oval table
Upright chair (up C)
Window-seat. *On it:* squab
Stool
Desk. *On it:* fountain pen, Biro, box of cigarettes, lighter, ash-
tray, telephone, Jane's dark glasses, blotter, inkstand,
scribbling pad
In drawer: 6 registered envelopes, 2 £5 notes
Under desk: waste-paper basket
Desk chair. *On it:* cushion
Armchair
Upright chair (R)
Built-in shelves. *On them:* 4 decorative china vases of good quality
Bureau with trick movable corner piece. *On it:* clock. *In it:* sheaf
of bills

 Standard lamp
 Chandelier
 Window curtains
 Carpet on floor
 Light switch below door up L
 On landing: upright chair
 pedestal
 Bell-push below door
 Electric socket in skirting board down L
Window closed
Window curtains open
Light fittings off
Door closed

Set:　*Above door up* L: Caxton's bag. *In it:* rag for packing

Off stage:　Keys wrapped in paper (CATHERINE)
 Rubber plant (JANE)
 Carrier bag. *In it:* stole (JANE)
 Carrier bag. *In it: crème de menthe* (JANE)
 Carrier bag. *In it:* dressing (JANE)
 String of onions (PHILIP)
 Cakestand. *On it:* cake, sandwiches, chocolate biscuits, knife
 (SUSAN)
 Tray. *On it:* pot of tea, milk, sugar, 3 cups, saucers and tea-
 spoons, 3 napkins, dish of muffins (ROSE)
 Receipt (ROSE)
 Dressmaker's dummy (PHILIP)

Personal:　CAXTON: handkerchief, glasses, watch, visiting-card, torch,
 coin, magnifying glass, wallet with notes
 SUSAN: handbag, gloves
 CATHERINE: spectacles, pencil
 JANE: handbag. *In it:* compact
 PHILIP: lighter
 FIONA: handbag. *In it:* cheque-book

ACT II

Strike:　Fallen mirror
 Stole
 Crème de menthe
 Carrier bags
 Registered envelopes
 Lighter
 Upright chair from R
 Vase of flowers from console table

Move: Sofa to C, facing down L
   Armchair down R to down L
   Table LC to R of armchair
   Chair L to up R of table

Set: *On console table:* ornament
  On wall over console table: small mirror
  On sofa: cushion from desk chair
  On table L: screwdriver, pliers, penknife, electric plug, Jane's evening
   bag, box of 50 cigarettes, scissors
  On desk: £100 cheque, address book, papers, etc. *In drawer:* loose
   papers
  On shelves R: ornaments
  On floor down L: electric radiator
  Nest of three tables up R
Window closed
Window curtains closed
Door open
Light fittings on

Off stage: Tray. *On it:* 3 saucers, 4 small cups (ROSE)
    Table-lighter (CATHERINE)
    Roll of insulating tape (PHILIP)
    Dish of olives (ROSE)
    Vase of flowers (SUSAN)
    Box of chocolates (JANE)
    2 saucers (JANE)
    Brief-case (CAXTON)
    Parcel. *In it:* wrapped Elvas plums (BRIGETTE)
    Cocktail (PHILIP)
    Packet of savings (ROSE)
    Tray. *On it:* 2 cocktails (SUSAN)
    Coin (ROSE)

Personal: CATHERINE: watch
   CAXTON: cheque-book
   BRIGETTE: gloves, outsize handbag. *In it:* bottle of alcohol,
    tissues, silk shawl, cheque-book, Biro

ACT III

Strike: Everything from table L
   Flowers and cigarettes from desk
   Electric fire
   Nest of tables

Set: *On table* L: box of cigarettes, ashtray
 On desk: scissors, table-lighter, ashtray
 In bureau cupboard: notebook, *crème de menthe,* glasses

Reset: Sofa to C

Window closed
Window curtains open
Door closed
Light fittings off

Off stage: Parcel. *In it:* emeralds (ROSE)
 Bunch of red roses tied with red ribbon (JANE)
 Small grip (JANE)
 Small grip (CATHERINE)

Personal: CATHERINE: watch
 JANE: handbag. *In it:* cheroots
 CAXTON: lighter, tweezers, silk handkerchief, jeweller's eyeglass
 FIONA: handbag. *In it:* long cigarette-holder, cotton-wool
 BRIGETTE: handbag. *In it:* bottle of alcohol, tissues

LIGHTING PLOT

Property fittings required: standard lamp, chandelier, **radiator**
Interior. A drawing-room. The same scene throughout

THE MAIN ACTING AREAS are C, up LC, at a sofa LC and at a desk RC

THE APPARENT SOURCES OF LIGHT are in daytime, a large bay window
up R; and at night, a chandelier pendant C and a standard lamp
up R

ACT I. Afternoon

To open:	Effect of spring sunshine	
	Fittings off	
	Strip outside door L, on	
Cue 1	JANE switches the chandelier on and off	(Page 8)
	Snap chandelier in and out	
Cue 2	CAXTON switches on standard lamp	(Page 11)
	Snap in standard lamp	
Cue 3	JANE: ". . . two hundred pounds."	(Page 27)
	Snap out standard lamp	

ACT II. Evening

To open:	Effect of dull daylight outside window	
	Fittings on	
	Strip outside door L, on	

No cues

ACT III. Afternoon

To open:	Effect of spring sunshine	
	Fittings off	
	Strip outside door L, on	
Cue 4	PHILIP switches on standard lamp	(Page 68)
	Snap in standard lamp	

EFFECTS PLOT

ACT I

Cue 1   ROSE: ". . . up those stairs."   (Page 5)
Telephone rings

Cue 2   CATHERINE: ". . . expecting her any time."   (Page 6)
Sound of door slam

ACT II

No cues

ACT III

Cue 3   CATHERINE: ". . . come in and . . ."   (Page 53)
Door slam